RESISTING HAPPINESS

MATTHEW KELLY

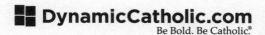
DynamicCatholic.com
Be Bold. Be Catholic.®

RESISTING HAPPINESS

Hardcover ISBN-978-1-942611-91-2
Paperback ISBN-978-1-942611-92-9
Audiobook ISBN-978-1-942611-99-8
Ebook ISBN-978-1-942611-93-6

Cover Design by Jessie Sayward Bright
Interior Design by Jenny Miller

The Dynamic Catholic Institute
5081 Olympic Blvd • Erlanger, Kentucky 41018
Phone: 1–859–980–7900
Email: info@DynamicCatholic.com

For more information visit:
www.DynamicCatholic.com
First Edition

[1]

Printed in the United States of America

Table of Contents

Note: The names of certain people throughout this book have been changed to respect their privacy.

Resistance

The alarm clock goes off. It's time to get out of bed. This is your first decision of the day. Will you get out of bed or hit the snooze button? You press the snooze button and roll over.

What just happened? No big deal, right? Wrong. You just lost the first battle of the day. Resistance just kicked your butt. Resistance has broken your will before you've even gotten out of bed. You will most likely be its slave for the rest of the day.

I have been battling resistance my whole life. As we get a little further into this book I think you will discover you have been too. What is resistance? It's that sluggish feeling of not wanting to do something that you know is good for you, it's the inclination to do something that you unabashedly know is *not* good for you, and it's everything in between. It's the desire and tendency to delay something you should be doing right now.

Do you ever feel like you are your own worst enemy? Have you ever thought you could accomplish great things if only you weren't so busy with so many little things? Do you struggle to make decisions with confidence? Are you tired of setting goals and not accomplishing them? Do you procrastinate? Are you afraid to say what you really think and feel? Then this book is for you.

If you've ever tried to accomplish anything worthwhile, then you've been face-to-face with resistance. You may not have called it by that name in the past, but I suspect you will in the future. It helps to call it by its name. In every moment of every day, resistance is there, waiting to pounce.

The hardest war to win is one you don't even realize you are fighting, and the hardest enemy to defeat is the one you don't even know exists. Every day you are at war with resistance.

Make no mistake, resistance is your enemy. It will not quietly go away and leave you alone. You have to slay it like a dragon, and you have to slay it anew each day.

How does resistance manifest? It wears a thousand masks, many of which are so effective we don't even recognize resistance is behind them. Laziness, procrastination, fear, doubt, instant gratification, self-loathing, indecision, escapism, pride, self-deception, friction, tension, and self-sabotage are just some of the ways resistance manifests its ugly self in our lives and causes us to settle for so much less than God has imagined for us. You cannot become the-best-version-of-yourself unless you wake up every morning ready to slay resistance. It stands between you and the person God created you to be. Resistance stands between you and happiness.

You have to break through resistance in order to accomplish even the smallest tasks. I catch myself in a battle with resistance several times a day.

Here's a simple example:

I sit down to write, but instead I start checking my e-mail or thinking about what snacks will be *required* to write something great. This is resistance at work. Sure, I am an accomplished author and have written twenty books that have sold millions of copies, but just like every college student who sits down to write a paper, I will have to slay resistance in order to even get started. The thing about resistance is that it is so simple, so ordinary—and so paralyzing if we are not mindful of it.

This is why most people who start writing a book never finish it. We all know people who are writing a book. I get requests from people all the time to help them get the book they are writing published. They are very keen to speak about the publishing process right now. I always say to them, "Focus first on writing your book. When your manuscript is finished and ready for a professional editor to look at, send me a copy, and then we can talk about publishing options." More than 95 percent of them I never hear from again. Resistance gets the better of them.

Imagine all the books that are unwritten because of resistance. I wonder if Mozart or Beethoven had an unwritten symphony, or if Picasso and Monet died with their greatest work inside them because of resistance. I wonder how many diseases have not been cured because resistance got between the scientist and the cure. I wonder how many things never got invented because inventors succumbed to resistance. How many men and women didn't become saints because of resistance? Resistance is a slayer of dreams.

Looking back on today, where did you encounter resistance? It was there, wasn't it? In fact, if you really sat down and analyzed your day, you would discover that many times throughout the day you were in a tussle with resistance.

We all battle resistance daily: popes and presidents; kings, queens, and the working class; the CEO and the janitor; the rich and the poor; the educated and the uneducated; the young and the old. Nobody gets to escape the battle with resistance.

The first goal of this book is simply to give resistance a name. Once you name it, you see it differently. Things that we cannot name tend to build in mystery and become dangerous. Simply naming, defining, and learning to recognize resistance in the moments of our days causes it to lose most of its power over us. It is no longer a mystery because we have named it.

When aspiring authors contact me for advice, I always ask them a series of questions about their book. One of those questions is: What is the promise of your book? They usually look at me and wonder what on earth I am talking about. But to me, every book makes a promise. A great book delivers on its promise and an average book does not. Learning to overcome resistance is one of life's essential lessons, and the promise of this book.

The first lesson is that you never defeat resistance once and for all. It is a daily battle.

⭐ **KEY POINT**

Resistance stands between you and happiness.

⚡ **ACTION STEP**

Write down every time you encounter resistance for a week.

②

Your Quest for Happiness

We resist all sorts of things for all sorts of reasons. But perplexingly, it usually comes down to this: We resist happiness. It's perplexing because at the same time we have an insatiable desire for happiness.

I have been resisting happiness my whole life. I see it clearly now, but I didn't always. I caught glimpses of it here and there throughout my life, but it wasn't until I was forty that I really recognized the patterns. What is most disturbing and humbling is that even now that I know how resistance works, how to recognize it, and how to overcome it, there are still daily instances when I allow it to win.

We tend to see these patterns in other people's lives with much more clarity than we see them in our own. For years I have observed people resisting happiness. We have seen it in the lives of our family, friends, and colleagues. We have all seen patterns of laziness and procrastination cripple people personally and professionally. We have all seen patterns of fear and self-loathing turn beautiful, intelligent people into a shadow of their true selves. We have all sat by while people we love sabotage their chances at success and happiness over and over again. These are the patterns that we see in people's lives, patterns that make us wonder why.

Then there are the times when we watch as someone we love, against the advice of everyone in his or her inner circle, does something monumentally stupid. We wonder to ourselves, "Why would anybody do something so stupid?" The answer is universal and disarmingly simple: People do stupid things because they mistakenly believe those stupid things will make them happy.

This is the paradox that surrounds our quest for happiness: We know the things that will make us happy, but we don't always do them.

We know how to unleash happiness in our lives, but we don't. Why? Resistance. We are all on a quest for happiness, but resistance gets the better of us.

I know the people, things, behaviors, and experiences that make me happy. It is no surprise to anyone, I suspect, that these are the same people, things, behaviors, and experiences that help me become a-better-version-of-myself.

Working hard makes me happy. And there is no work that brings me more joy than writing. Writing makes me happy, and at the end of a good day of writing everything is better in my world. Still, every time I sit down to write, before I can even get a word down, I have to battle and slay resistance.

A morning walk makes me happy. It clears my mind, fires up my metabolism, and gets the endorphins moving through my body. There is no comparison between a day with a morning walk and one without it. And yet, resistance fills my mind with a hundred excuses at that moment of decision each and every morning.

Sitting down for a few minutes of prayer and reflection at the beginning of the day makes me happy. It gives me the clarity, focus, perspective, and gratitude I need to make the most of the day. But almost every day I am tempted to put it off until later or skip it altogether. Why? The allure of action, the temptation to believe that going somewhere or doing something is urgent. This is one of my first struggles with resistance each day, and resistance knows that this is the most significant battle of the day. If resistance can keep me from praying, it will win many more battles throughout the day.

There are a dozen other examples, but starting my day with prayer, taking a walk, and jumping straight into my work is a bulletproof recipe for me to exponentially increase my chances of having a fabulous day.

What makes you happy? Do you know? Before we jump into that question, a better place to start might be with this question: Are you happy?

Give yourself a happiness score between one and ten over the past three months. Don't base it on how you feel today or over the past week; you might just be having a bad week. Three months gives us a better look. What's your happiness score? Scribble it somewhere on this page.

Most people think they are reasonably happy, and most people yearn to be happier. So, let's do something about that. Let's increase your happiness score. I am certain that what I am about to share with you in these pages is going to flood your life with happiness, and so much more.

It's time to stop resisting happiness. It's time to stop destroying our own happiness. We do it in so many ways. Do you worry about things you have no control over? Worry destroys happiness. Do you compare yourself with others in an unhealthy way? Comparison is a destroyer of happiness. Do you cling to bad relationships? Bad relationships destroy our happiness. Do you have a lot of self-doubt, or even self-loathing? They are destroyers of happiness. Do you buy things you can't afford and don't need? Debt is a destroyer of happiness and a creator of stress. Gossip, laziness, fear, excuses, negative thinking, ingratitude, and jealousy are all destroyers of happiness.

You are on a quest for happiness. Working out what makes you happy is essential, but so is working out what destroys your happiness. In order to do this, let's explore why we all have such an ongoing desire for happiness.

⭐ **KEY POINT**
Find out what really makes you happy.

⚡ **ACTION STEP**
Identify three activities that increase your happiness. Write them down.

---

(3)

Making Sense of Everything

Do you know anyone who doesn't want to be happy? You want to be happy, and I want to be happy. Your boyfriend or girlfriend wants to be happy, your husband or wife wants to be happy, and if you have children, they want to be happy too. Your friends want to be happy, and your colleagues and customers at work want to be happy. Everyone wants to be happy, and we are all chasing happiness in our own way. It starts when we are very young.

When we are children, we think to ourselves, "Oh, if only I could have that toy, I would be happy." But then we get that toy and after a while we realize that a toy is not going to satisfy our desire for happiness. So we turn our attention toward something else, perhaps a bike. We tell ourselves, "If I ever get that bike, I will be happy." We get the bike and of course the yearning for happiness is still not satisfied.

As we get a little older and social interactions become more important we tend to attach our hope for happiness to friendship. Now we think to ourselves, "If she became my best friend, I would be happy forever." But our desire for happiness cannot be fulfilled in this way either. No one person can satisfy our immense desire for happiness. And it is not fair to attach that hope to any one person. So many relationships have died under the weight of this misplaced expectation.

In our adolescent years we tend to turn our attention toward pleasure. We tell ourselves, "If I have this pleasure or that pleasure, or all the pleasures at the same time, then I will be happy." But pleasure is a poor substitute for the happiness we desire. It is fleeting and we yearn for something that is lasting.

Our attention in early adulthood turns toward accomplishment. We think to ourselves, "I know the answer now. If I can accomplish something great, I will stop feeling empty and dissatisfied, and I will be happy forever." Maybe we do and maybe we don't accomplish something great, but regardless, the yearning for a happiness that is higher or deeper continues.

At this point most people just cycle back through all the same things, thinking that more of something or more of everything is the answer to their insatiable desire for happiness. So they chase more things, more money, more pleasure, more of the "right" friends, and more accomplishments. But they end up dissatisfied and wondering what on earth will satisfy this incredible desire for happiness. The answer is nothing.

Nothing on earth can satisfy your desire for happiness.

The reason is very simple: You have a God-size hole. You cannot fill it with things, money, status, power, sex, drugs, alcohol, other people, experiences, or accomplishments. Only God can fill the hole. Throw all the money and possessions in the world into the hole and you will find it is still empty and you are still yearning for something more. Throw an Oscar, a Pulitzer, a Grammy or two, ten or twenty million dollars, and a Nobel Peace Prize into the hole and it will still seem empty.

We often make the mistake of hoping that certain people or things will fill the hole, but sooner or later most of us come to realize that only God can fill that hole that represents all our deepest longings. The hole is bigger than anything this life has to offer, but allowing God to fill it will make everything this life has to offer better.

We yearn for happiness because we are created for happiness. "The desire for God is written in the human heart because man is created by God and for God; and God never ceases to draw man to himself. Only in God will he find the truth and happiness he never stops searching for (*CCC*, 27)." This is the opening point of the first chapter of the *Catechism of the Catholic Church*.

What does this mean for you?
  • The desire for God is written on your heart. It cannot be erased;
  • You are created by God and for God;
  • God never ceases to draw you to him; and
  • You will only find the truth and happiness you are looking for in God.

The whole meaning and purpose of your existence is wrapped up in God. Separated from him, you and your life lose their meaning.

About a week before Easter this year I overheard a conversation between my eldest son, Walter, who is six years old, and my daughter, Isabel, who is four.

"You are too wrapped up in Jesus, Isabel!"

"Well, Easter is all about Jesus, so it's good to be wrapped up in him," Isabel replied.

"I like Jesus, but I am more interested in the chocolate eggs and the chocolate bunnies."

Wow! There it is. Too often we are more interested in something other than Jesus, something other than the happiness that God wants to freely give us.

Who or what is at the center of your life?

It is only by placing God at the center of everything that we can make sense of life. When we place something or someone else at the center of our lives we set ourselves up for a gnawing dissatisfaction.

Placing anything at the center of our lives other than God creates a disorientation that leads to immense confusion. This confusion has a firm grip on so many people today. Again, we often see this more clearly in other people's lives than we do in our own.

If you want to make sense of everything, place God at the center of your life. Have you ever really tried it? What do you have to lose?

⭐ **KEY POINT**

It is only by placing God at the center of everything that we can make sense of life.

⚡ **ACTION STEP**

Place God at the center of the next decision you make by choosing not what you want or what is most advantageous to you, but what you honestly feel God wants you to do.

Resisting God

When we resist happiness we are really resisting God. God is happiness. Think about that. The definition of resist is "to withstand, strive against, or oppose." To oppose God is a fool's errand. Only the insane and egomaniacal would resist God, and yet, I suspect we all fall into both those categories from time to time. Consider that idea for a moment. Don't just read through it. Reflect on the insanity of trying to resist God.

What's fascinating to me is that even though the quest for happiness is one of the defining themes of every person's life, God wants us to be happy even more than we want to be happy ourselves.

Have you ever wanted something good for someone more than he wanted it for himself?

This is the dilemma that every parent, teacher, pastor, coach, and leader faces. We see what is possible for our children, students, parishioners, players, and those we lead, but we cannot always help them to see those possibilities for themselves.

My consulting company has a large coaching practice. We have life coaches to help people develop a strategic plan for their lives. We have business coaches to help entrepreneurs grow their businesses. And we have executive coaches to help corporate leaders gain perspective on the biggest challenges facing their businesses and organizations. It's amazing how life changing this type of coaching can be. Do some get more out of it than others? Yes. Why? Some people are more committed and engaged in the process.

Whenever I speak to the coaches, I warn them about one scenario. "You are going to be tempted to judge yourself as a coach by how well your participants perform. That's a mistake and it leads to a bad place. Your participants' successes and failures are their own. You cannot take credit for their successes, and you cannot take the blame for their failures. Your job is to coach them well by faithfully following the coaching program. Otherwise you will end up crossing a line that a coach should never cross. You will find yourself in a place where you want it for them more than they want it for themselves. Then you will make your first mistake. You will do something for them that they should be doing for themselves. You will think you are helping them, but it is a lie and you know it. Your job is to empower those you coach; when you do for them what they should be doing for themselves, you create entitlement and dependency rather than empowerment. It is incredibly frustrating when you see amazing possibilities for the people you are coaching, and you want it more for them than they want it for themselves. Don't give in to that frustration!"

God wants you to be happy even more than you want it yourself.

Imagine how frustrated God is with us, seeing all that is possible and knowing how we squander so much. But he will not cross the line. He will not step over your free will. God wants to empower you for mission. He has put you in this world for a specific mission, but first he has to prepare you.

God wants heaven for you even more than you want it for yourself.

When we resist happiness, we resist God and the-very-best-version-of-ourselves. To resist God is to resist our very truest selves. When we resist happiness we place a barrier between ourselves and God, a barrier between ourselves and the incredible people God created us to be, a barrier between ourselves and the wonderful life God dreamed for us before we were in our mothers' wombs.

It's time to stop resisting happiness. It's time to slay resistance.

⭐ **KEY POINT**
When we resist God we resist happiness.

⚡ **ACTION STEP**
Learn to recognize when you want something for others more than they want it for themselves.

---

(5)

Life Is Messy

Life is messy. When I first started speaking and writing, I was so young—nineteen years old. Even though I lived through it, it seems impossible to me now that I did what I did at that age. How did I get from being that nineteen-year-old in Sydney, Australia, to this forty-two-year-old living in the United States? How did so much get accomplished? The truth is, I don't know. I can't understand how it all happened. I don't know why it happened to me.

I do know this: In those early years, I had no idea that life was so messy. In some ways I suppose that was a good thing, because if I had known how difficult, heartbreaking, and messy this path would be, I'm not sure I would have had the courage to set out in the beginning. Perhaps that is why God only reveals our journey to us one step at a time.

In others ways, my naïveté about the messiness of life limited my ability to reach people during those early years. In order to speak deep into people's lives, you have to have a sense of their heartache, of what keeps them awake at night. I was too young and too inexperienced to know much about these things.

A huge part of coming alongside people and helping them discover who they are and what they are here for is mercy. And a big part of mercy is simply being with people in their pain and suffering, holding them physically or spiritually, even if there is nothing else you can do for them. But when I first set out I was too spiritually immature to know this.

Many years later, when I was first diagnosed with cancer, I remember walking out of the doctor's office. It was a bright, sunny day, and the light was blinding. I was in a daze. Things were spinning. I had to sit in my car and steady myself for a couple of minutes before driving home. But the thing that struck me the most was that everyone around was going about their day. They had no idea what was happening inside me. That experience changed me forever. It changed the way I relate with family and friends. It changed the way I lead and manage people. It changed the way I speak and write.

The lesson I learned was that someone can look perfectly fine, but you never know what is going on inside—and everyone has something going on inside.

Most people can hide it pretty well and get on with whatever the day requires of them so that they can support their families and raise their kids, or keep their schools, churches, businesses, or hospitals running. But it doesn't change the fact that each of us in our own way is grappling with something.

One of my great passions is reading biographies and autobiographies. I find it fascinating to see how people's lives unfold, especially as they strive to honor their talent in the midst of extraordinary worldly success. A few years ago I was reading Bob Dylan's autobiography *Chronicles*. Dylan was talking about his grandmother—his mother's mother—who lived with his family when he was a child: "She was filled with nobility and goodness . . . and told me once, be kind because everyone you'll ever meet is fighting a hard battle." Wow. What a fabulous insight.

"Everyone you'll ever meet is fighting a hard battle." What hard battle are you fighting?

What hard battle are the people who live under the same roof as you wrestling with? What hard battle are the people you work with fighting?

When we recognize that someone else is fighting a hard battle, we tend to rise to the occasion. It brings the best out in us, and compassion and generosity begin to flow. So next time somebody is upsetting you, frustrating, annoying, or ignoring you, take a deep breath and remember that she is fighting her own hard battle. Allow the greatness of your humanity to rise up within you, and act with compassion. Smile, be warm, pray for her, and move on quietly.

Jesus gave us the perfect example as he was being nailed to the cross, when he called out, "Father, forgive them; for they know not what they do" (Luke 23:34).

Life is messy. Birth and death, fear and pain, disease and suffering, hunger and abuse, addiction and betrayal, corruption and exploitation, disappointment and failure, injustice and broken dreams—there is no question, life can be very messy indeed. Often we are quite good at avoiding the mess. But as children of God we are called to go looking for the mess and make a difference in some way—large or small—according to the gifts that have been entrusted to us.

At Dynamic Catholic we invite members of our Ambassador's Club to send in prayer requests. Each day we have Mass at the chapel in our office and we pray especially for all our Ambassadors, but particularly for these intentions. Each week, wherever I am, someone on the team e-mails me a list of all the prayer requests, so that I can pray personally over these requests. I can rarely get through four or five of them before my eyes begin to fill with tears.

It is amazing what ordinary people are carrying around with them each day. Here are some recent prayer requests:

- Please pray for my sister Delores, who has a type of leukemia that is not curable; my sister-in-law, Amy, who is trying to recover from cancer; and for our priest, Monsignor Higley, who has breathed new life into our parish, so that he continues to bring the energy and devotion needed here.
- My assistant and friend found out her daughter, who's in college, was raped. She is devastated. Then three weeks ago her husband had a stroke and they found out he is suffering some form of muscular dystrophy.
- My nineteen-year-old daughter suffers from depression and anxiety; please pray for her.
- Please add the Lotarski family to your prayers. My cousin JP and his wife Julie's six-week-old baby girl, London Ann, just had emergency heart surgery this weekend. Her lungs are filling with fluid and they don't know if she will pull through. They tried for five years to have children and

were so overjoyed when they became pregnant and when London was born.

- We need your prayers. Both my father-in-law, Mike (stage 4), and cousin-in-law Joseph (stage 3B) are battling cancer at the moment. Ricky also has cystic fibrosis and already had lung treatment two years ago. My husband has been job hunting for over a year and has not yet found a job.

- After returning from a retreat last March, my eighteen-year-old daughter let us know that at the age of eight she was sexually abused for two years by a former neighbor. She has buried this for nine years. She was in a deep depression. She did not go away to college but has been in constant therapy and is making progress; however, two things have happened: She has turned away from the Church, and she is now questioning her own sexuality—which they say is normal.

- I am looking for love but this time I want someone who is a devoted Catholic man. All the people I have met are not Catholic, and those who say they are Catholic do not practice. It sounds like a silly prayer request, but I have lost my drive and faith in God because of so many disappointments.

- I was just diagnosed with a cancerous tumor in my colon. We just lost our home, its contents, and our pets in a fire. We are just trying to recover from all of this, and we need strength. Thank you for your prayers.

We receive thousands of prayer requests. This is just a small sample from recently. It is incredible what people are carrying around inside.

Some weeks I pick up the pages of prayer requests and start reading and praying, and I become overwhelmed by a deep sadness—and I am just *reading* about the things people are dealing with.

Life is messy.

Several years ago, I was visiting a church and in the bulletin they were inviting people to adopt a less fortunate family for Christmas. I thought this was a fabulous idea, so I sent an e-mail to the person coordinating it and agreed to adopt a family for Christmas that year.

A few weeks later, the church sent us the information about the family, names, and ages of the children, and a wish list they had invited the children to put together. Also included was some background information about the family, and it was heartbreaking.

This has become part of our Christmas tradition as a family, and it seems each year the stories get sadder. This is what was passed along about the family we were asked to adopt this past Christmas:

Courtney and Dawn, thirty-four years old. Their children: Kiasia (12), CJ (5), and Arirone (3).

Dawn is battling serious cancer. Courtney cannot work due to his wife's illness, her needs, and the children's needs. The children have excellent school attendance.

The cancer started in Dawn's colon over a year and a half ago. She has been on feeding tubes since then, and will always be on them going forward. The cancer returned and they had to remove other organs.

Courtney has been taught how to insert and remove the various tubes for his wife. He does not want her to go to a nursing home.

They have recently moved homes and schools to lower their rent bill.

Dawn has no colon and no stomach. There is a new procedure available, a stomach transplant. But in order to qualify for this procedure you have to be five years cancer-free. Dawn is two years cancer-free, and she can only live for two more years on the tubes.

Courtney is going to send the kids' wish lists, but we found out that the two girls sleep together in a twin bed. They are in serious need of other furniture items in addition to decent beds and bedding for the children and the parents.

Where do you start? To say that their life together is messy is an understatement of monumental proportions. I went home and I hugged my wife and said, "Let's make this an incredible Christmas for this family!" Then I went around the house, looking for my children one by one, and I hugged them long and tight and told them how much I love them.

Life is messy, and it is not enough just to talk about the mess. We are each called to do something about it.

It's time to confront our own mess, how it affects us, and how our mess affects others. But it is also time to reach out to others who have a mess greater or smaller than our own and be with them in their mess.

When I reflect on Christmas, one of the ideas that has longevity practically and spiritually is the fact that God decided to put himself right in the middle of our mess. The world was a mess. It was our mess, not his mess. He didn't need to come and be with us, among us. He could have redeemed us in an infinite number of other ways. But he chose to put himself in our midst, in the middle of our mess. He didn't say, "This is your mess; clean it up yourself." Rather, in an infinite expression of divine mercy he came to be with us in our mess.

When the modern-day Pharisees see the drug addict, they say, "She needs to quit doing that stuff." When they see the homeless, they say, "We need to get these people off the streets." When they see the un-employed, they say, "He should get a job." And when someone stops them on the street asking for money, they say, "If I gave him money he would probably just spend it on drugs and booze," or "If I give her money I will just be encouraging her to continue asking for more."

Life is messy and we are called to put ourselves in the middle of the mess and work to make a difference, however small. We are all carrying a heavy load, fighting a hard battle, but so is every person we encounter in this mystery we call life. Jesus invites us to "take up [our] cross daily" (Luke 9:23). And some days we are called to take up someone else's cross also, so he can catch his breath, have a short rest, or simply have his faith in the goodness of humanity restored.

Resistance will tell you that the problems are too many and that you will never make a difference. Ignore it. Resistance is a liar.

Don't let it make you feel helpless in the face of life's mess. Don't listen to resistance when it comes wearing the mask of discouragement. Never give in to discouragement. You are not alone. You are not helpless. Take some small action. Resistance hates action. Turn to God in prayer. Resistance hates it when we turn to God and trust in him. Reach out to somebody and say, "I am discouraged," and just by saying the words you will begin to cast out that discouragement and regain your hope.

Let's decide together, right here and right now, to do something about the mess in our own lives, and whenever possible the mess in other people's lives. In order to do that, we have to learn how to break through resistance. Resistance is like a wall that we have to break through in order to begin anything. Resistance loves inaction. That's why as soon as you decide to act, it raises its ugly head in a dozen ways to distract you.

Think about some part of your life that is messy. What positive step can you take this week, however small, to improve that mess? Resistance hates action. It wants you to sit around feeling helpless and getting discouraged. Take action and you will feel yourself begin to fill with hope again.

Life is messy, but nobody can take your hope from you. And if there is one thing that resistance hates, it is hope. So hold on to your hope no matter how messy life gets, and share it with everyone who crosses your path.

In the pages and chapters that follow I am going to share with you some of the key moments in my life when I resisted happiness and resisted God, and how even though it often seems I am taking three steps forward and two steps back, God has patiently waited for me to overcome resistance. Try not to judge me. Many books can be written without revealing too much personally. But as I began working on this book it became clear that the most effective way to teach people about resistance is to let them deep into my own life and my own struggles. This is something I have never been very comfortable with. So I just ask that you walk with me gently, accept my brokenness as part of my journey, and pray for me as I am praying for you to get better every day at slaying resistance.

As you read my story, reflect on your own. Take note of the moments in your life when you were challenged to grow. Be mindful also of any decisions you have made that leave you in need of healing now. What's most important here is not my story, but yours. If in some way my story can help you discover your own in a new way, then that is a beautiful grace. As you read about my resistance, try to reflect on the times when you have met or failed to overcome it, and the times God has called you subtly or not so subtly to become the-best-version-of-yourself.

⭐ **KEY POINT**

Everyone you meet is fighting a hard battle and carrying a heavy load.

⚡ **ACTION STEP**

Be gentle with the people who cross your path. If someone is grumpy or rude, if someone makes a mistake or does something wrong, give her the benefit of the doubt. You never know what she is carrying around inside.

Something Is Missing

Do you ever have the sense that something is missing in your life? We all do from time to time. Most people push it aside fairly quickly, because we are afraid of where it might lead. But we really should pay a little more attention to our dissatisfaction.

Push it aside, ignore it, pretend it isn't there, but it won't go away. And the more you ignore it the more restless you will become. We have all watched a friend who needs to make a decision but refuses to confront the situation. He pretends that all is well, but everyone around him can see he is becoming more and more restless.

Perhaps a student has an important exam coming up, but he doesn't take the time to study. As the exam gets closer his anxiety increases because he knows he isn't prepared, yet at the same time, he refuses to study. Resistance has a firm grip on him. All the energy he should be using to study is being used on anxiety. Until he decides to sit down and study, the anxiety will continue to grow.

It's okay to be dissatisfied. Being dissatisfied and pretending that we are not is the kind of lie that leads

to spiritual and physical illness. Our dissatisfaction is trying to lead us to something better, or something different altogether.

It is time to start listening to what God is saying to us through our dissatisfaction. I want to encourage you to pay a little more attention to that sense that something is missing in your life. This quiet discontent is creating restlessness in you for a reason.

Restlessness is something I am very familiar with. Most days I experience it in some form or another. It drives my creativity and gives birth to ideas. But each day the restlessness needs to be tamed so that I can actually do something. Otherwise I would just sit around coming up with ideas all the time. Nothing would get done, and I certainly wouldn't ever finish anything.

But beyond these daily experiences with restlessness, there have been a handful of extraordinary encounters with it that have left their mark on my life. When I was fifteen years old I had a growing sense that something was missing. I was doing well in school, I excelled at sports, I had a wonderful girlfriend, and I had started a couple of businesses. I grew up in a very entrepreneurial family. Sitting at the dinner table each night was basically like attending classes for an MBA. So by the time I was a sophomore in high school I was making more money than my teachers, and I remember thinking, "There must be more to life than getting good grades, having a job, and making money." My heart was restless. I knew something was missing, but I didn't know what to do about it. I had this nagging sense that there simply must be more to life, but I didn't know what it was or where to find it. So, I did what most of us do. I tried to ignore the feelings, but the nagging restlessness persisted.

If you sense that something is missing in your life, stop ignoring it. Start paying attention to it. God is trying to tell you something.

✪ KEY POINT

It's time to start listening to what God is saying to us through our dissatisfaction.

⚡ ACTION STEP

Don't pretend to be happy and satisfied when you are not.

The Big Question

Before we go on I would just like to say that if you have read some of my other books you will find I have repeated a couple of stories here. Over the years I have used stories about the early years of my spiritual conversion in books and speeches, but because I have never put them all in one place or in chronological order, I often get questions. If you have read one of the stories before, I encourage you not to skip through it, but to try to go deeper into it. Ask yourself, "Am I living the lesson of this story?"

A few weeks after I first recognized my restlessness, I was at a barbecue one Sunday afternoon with some of my mates when I bumped into a family friend. He was about fifteen years older than I was, so he was hanging out with the adults and I was talking to my friends. But after about an hour he came over to me and struck up a conversation.

"How are you, Matthew?" he asked.

"Fine."

"How is school going?"

"Fine."

"I see you made the varsity soccer team!"

"Yep."

For five or ten minutes he kept trying to engage me in conversation, gently probing into different areas of my life with his questions.

His name was John and he was a doctor. Good doctors know how to ask the right questions. Where does it hurt? When did it start hurting? What happened around that time? If I apply pressure here, does it hurt? What about here?

Each question and each answer that afternoon led him closer to his diagnosis. Finally, he paused briefly, looked deep into my eyes, and said, "You're not happy, are you, Matthew?" He knew it and I knew it. At first I was defensive and ashamed to admit it. But there are moments when our lives flood with unexpected grace. This was one of them, and I began to speak with him about the restlessness I was experiencing.

I don't know what I expected him to say. But it wasn't what he said. "Why don't you try stopping by church for ten minutes on the way to school each morning?"

My brothers and I walked to school each morning. He knew that. And we had to pass by the chapel, which was right at the entrance to our high school campus.

I was polite. I listened and smiled, but inside I was thinking to myself, "What sort of religious fanatic is this guy?" He talked about how this would change my life and I remember wondering, "How is ten minutes each day in an empty church going to change my life?"

At the time I had no idea, but resistance was at work. In the coming weeks I kept busy.

Resistance loves keeping us busy with anything but the one thing that will most help us grow.

I threw myself into my studies, my sports, and my businesses with more energy than ever before. But the restlessness persisted.

Six weeks later I found myself wandering into church on the way to school. I crept quietly into the chapel and sat toward the back. At first I just looked around. I didn't know what to do. Nobody had ever taught me how to pray. Sure, I knew how to say the Our Father, Hail Mary, and Glory Be. But nobody had ever taught me how to just spend time with God.

After a few minutes I started to plan my day. Almost immediately I began to experience a peace and clarity. I think that was the first time in my life that I felt consciously peaceful. I liked it. At the time I didn't realize it, but my young soul was tired and hungry.

The next day I was eager to get back there. After a couple of weeks it just became part of my morning routine. Each morning I would sit toward the back of the church and walk through the events of the coming day in my mind.

It was a few weeks before resistance started rearing its ugly head again. I was happier than I had been in months, maybe ever, but resistance wouldn't let go. It suggested that missing prayer a day here and there wouldn't make a difference. But it did. When I didn't pray I could tell the difference. When I made the effort to spend those ten minutes in prayer, I was happier. I was a better person.

How could such a small thing make such a huge difference? The inner life—our relationship with God and spirituality—is the leaven that allows every other facet of our lives to rise. Without this inner life, our lives are flat.

Of course, after the initial euphoria I found that most days I had to fight the temptation to walk past the chapel and get on with my day.

It's insane when you think about it. I was resisting happiness. I'd like to say I broke through that temptation every day. But I didn't. Some days I slayed resistance, and other days it slayed me.

Several weeks later I was in the back of the church one morning and had finished planning my day. I was just sitting there thinking, and it occurred to me that planning my day wasn't really prayer. So, I began to speak to God about what was happening in my life and the things that were on my mind.

This mental conversation with God was a complete game changer for me. For the next couple of months it became my new routine. Every morning I would stop by church, sit toward the back, plan my day, and have a casual conversation with God about whatever was on my mind.

Then one day I had a problem. Well, not so much a problem as a decision I needed to make. I remember looking up toward the tabernacle and saying in my heart, "God, this is the situation . . . these are the circumstances. . . . What do you think I should do?"

It was a moment of surrender. That question changed my life. I call it the big question: "God, what do you think I should do?" It is quite simple, really. The moment we open ourselves up to God's plans is the moment miracles begin to happen in our lives.

Our lives change when our habits change. New habits bring new life.

⭐ KEY POINT

Prayer changes everything, and nothing ever really changes until we give daily prayer a place in our lives.

⚡ ACTION STEP

Ask God for his advice. Take ten minutes sometime today to sit with him in silence. Present to him the biggest question you are struggling with at this time in your life, and ask him, "God, what do you think I should do?"

(8)

Four Words

When was the last time you paused to really think about your life? Was it last week? Last month? Last year? Or has it been a few years? Very often when I ask people this question, I see them searching their minds for an answer, and then they will say things like, "I honestly cannot tell you. I mean, I think about things that are happening in my life, or decisions that I need to make, but I can't remember the last time I purposefully made time to think about my life and how I am living it."

We are all so busy. I meet up with friends who have retired from demanding full-time jobs, and they tell me they are busier than they have ever been. Resistance loves to keep us busy. When we are too busy to reflect on how we are living our lives, it is almost certain that we are not busy doing the right things.

There are four words that embody the challenge of the Christian life; we find them in the fifth line of the Our Father: _Thy will be done._ These four words present the greatest challenge of Christianity.

How do you react to these four words? What do they make you think? How do they make you feel? When you first read them, how did your body react?

It all depends on our image of God. If we see God as "far away," trying to control everything and everyone, we probably react to these words as an infringement on our personal freedom. If we see God as a loving father who wants good things for us even more than we want them for ourselves, who always has our best interests at heart, then we react very differently. For this reason, it is important that we constantly reflect upon our image of God. How we see God has an enormous impact on our lives. Our image of God is the lens through which we see ourselves, others, and the world. Our spirituality is particularly impacted by the way we see God. It is good to explore the assumptions we have about him from time to time—not incessantly, because that becomes harmful, but to step back from time to time and ask: What is my image of God? How do I see him? What are his attributes?

It may even be helpful to write these things down. Our image of God is so deeply ingrained in us, but it is easy for life and the world to corrupt that image. And a false or distorted view of God tends to distort our relationships, which are the foundation of life in this world.

When Jesus invites us to call God Father, he is inviting us to a very intimate relationship with God, and telling us that the transcendent God of the universe is concerned with the needs of each and every one of us. Jesus is constantly presenting a beautiful image of God. It is only in the context of this true image that we can fully embrace those four words: Thy will be done.

When I first started traveling and speaking, I spoke at a conference in Illinois. There were various vendors selling things and I noticed a framed picture of Noah's ark for a child's nursery. Along the bottom of the frame was etched, "Noah did everything that the Lord God commanded him to do." (Genesis 7:5) I bought it and for many years I had it hanging in my study, where I write. When Walter was born, I hung it above his crib. It has hung above Isabel's and Harry's cribs, and now it is there above Ralph's.

Whenever I see that picture and read those words, it is like an instant examination of conscience. It is not easy to walk with God. It is not easy to live as he commands us to live.

When was the last time you knew exactly what God was inviting you to do in a situation but you did the opposite? We all fall into this willful rejection of "Thy will be done." We become proud and arrogant and willful, and with our actions we scream, "*My* will be done!" But does it make us happy?

This has been going on for a long time. Adam and Eve took and ate the fruit in the garden. Cain killed his brother, Abel. Lot's wife looked back on Sodom and Gomorrah, directly disobeying the instructions God had given her through the angel. The Israelites rebelled against what God had said to them through Moses, and as a result were left wandering in the dessert for forty years. God asked Jonah to go to Ninevah, but he flat out refused to go. Samson was told not to reveal the source of his strength, but he told Delilah.

We live in a culture that says the meaning of life is to get what we want, and that when we get what we want, then we will be happy. We yearn for happiness because we were created for it, so we fall for the lie. We race off into

the world to get what we want, but sooner or later we all realize that getting what we want doesn't make us happy.

At least not in the way we thought it would. A few months after you get that car that you wanted your whole life, it is just a car, a means of transportation. Does it bring you some happiness? Yes. Does it please and pleasure you? Yes. But it doesn't bring you that deep and lasting satisfaction that you yearn for.

Every day we make dozens of decisions, some of them large and most of them small. God wants to help you become a phenomenal decision maker. He wants to set you on fire with passion and purpose. He wants your yes to be a passionate and enthusiastic YES, and your no to be a firm NO. It is so easy to become lukewarm, but he doesn't want that for you.

The thing about being lukewarm is nobody ever thinks they are. I have had people share all sorts of personal failings with me. They will tell me they have a problem with lust and pornography, with gluttony and overeating, with jealousy and judging others, but I have never had someone say to me, "I'm a not a generous person." And I have never had anyone say to me, "I've become lukewarm like those people God talks about vomiting out of his mouth."

The other thing about being lukewarm is that it is so easy to blend in. The lukewarm typically go to Mass every Sunday and give money to their parish and other charities. From the outside they appear to be committed Christians. But the lukewarm also tend to choose convenience and comfort over what is right and just. They rarely talk about God or their spiritual journey. Jesus is part of their lives, but he is not at the center of their lives. They are not willing to make sacrifices to grow spiritually. They almost never think about heaven, but are instead obsessed with the things of this world. They structure their lives so they never really have to trust God too much. The lukewarm watch television shows they know don't make them the-best-version-of-themselves, and swear, and drink far too much from time to time.

These are just a few characteristics of the lukewarm. But I think you will agree that this one paragraph paints a pretty clear picture. How do I know these things? I see them clearly because I have been there. I have been there so many times.

God doesn't want us to be lukewarm. He wants to set us on fire. And when we are on fire we have great clarity and become excellent decision makers.

If you have children, isn't this right at the core of what you want for them? You want your children to become really good decision makers. Wouldn't you have great peace of mind if this were so? God is the ultimate parent, and he wants you and me, his children, to become great decision makers. When was the last time you invited God into your decision-making process?

Think about all the people we seek advice from, and all the people who give us their unsolicited advice. Whom do you turn to for advice?

When did you last ask God to advise you about a big decision you had to make?

Decisions are the foundation of life. With each decision we choose order or chaos, clarity or confusion, life or death, with God or against God. We have already discussed the insanity of choosing against

God, but clearly it has been going on for a long time, and we do it ourselves every day in some small way. Every decision we make leads us either toward the peace and happiness we yearn for or away from it. Our decisions are the foundation of our lives. Saint Augustine famously wrote in *Confessions*, "Our hearts are restless until they rest in you Lord." Many saints and many sinners have found these words to be profoundly true.

God invites us into a deep life of prayer so that he can fill us with a peace that nobody can take from us. We all need something that nobody can take from us. God wants to fill you with a peace that cannot be shaken; a peace that is untouchable.

Surrender to these four words: Thy will be done. Invite God into the center of your decision-making process. Seek his will in all things. This is the road that leads to the happiness we desire. It is a happiness that is not fleeting or short-lived; it is lasting happiness in this changing world. The idea that we can find happiness outside of God's will is one of the most absurd ideas in history, and yet we each employ this concept in some way great or small every day of our lives.

✪ KEY POINT
These are the four words that embody the Christian challenge: Thy will be done.

⚡ ACTION STEP
Take a few minutes to reflect on your image of God. Write down the qualities that make up the way you see God. Try to trace each quality back to its roots in your life.

Are You Spiritually Healthy?

For more than twenty years I have been encouraging people to set aside ten minutes a day for quiet prayer. I advise them to put a Post-it note on their bathroom mirror that reads: "Ten Minutes a Day!" I often wonder how many people who heard this message made prayer a habit in their lives.

Sometimes people will say, "I've heard you speak three times and every time you mention that ten minutes a day idea!" I always ask them, "How many days last week did you spend ten minutes in quiet conversation with God?" That gets them thinking. Then they answer, usually vaguely and with some sort of excuse attached. So, I'm going to keep talking about it until we are all doing it, every day!

There are two reasons this theme keeps emerging in my work. First, because this habit of prayer changed my life. Second, because I know from personal experience how hard it is to keep the habit going.

This is my biggest battle with resistance each day. Resistance will fight me every time; it will never just let me sit down and begin my prayer. It will try to distract me and discourage me. It will do anything and everything to prevent me from doing my prayer.

And if resistance cannot get me not to pray, it will get me to delay, to put it off until later. Resistance knows that delaying my prayer is as good as a victory. Because I will either rush it or do it poorly later, or I will delay it further, putting it off at every opportunity all day long, and then not do it at all.

Always take your first opportunity each day to spend time in prayer.

The daily habit of prayer leads us to spiritual health. The more ingrained this habit becomes in our lives, the clearer we hear the voice of God. The clearer we hear the voice of God in our lives, the more likely we are to walk in his ways, honor his will, and experience the peace and happiness he yearns to fill us with.

Are you spiritually healthy? Are you alive spiritually? Are you thriving or are you just surviving? When we are spiritually healthy we tend to be focused, invigorated, patient, and generous. When we aren't healthy spiritually we tend to be irritable, restless, and discontented.

It's interesting how seldom we talk about spiritual health. If you think about all the focus we place on physical health, and the billions of dollars we spend trying to achieve it, and then consider how little we talk about spiritual health, it says so much about the state of our culture.

God wants to bless you with spiritual vitality. Developing this kind of spiritual vitality is like building a skyscraper: You start by going down. You dig deep, deep into the earth to create a foundation to support the huge structure. The higher you want to build the structure, the deeper you have to dig into the earth to begin with.

We all have an inner life. This consists of our thoughts and feelings, our hopes and dreams, our character and our relationship with God. We all have an outer life, which consists of the things we do, places we go, and things we build or own. We tend to focus on the outer life, but it is only a tiny fraction of our life. Much more takes place as part of the inner life. The outer life is an overflow of the inner life.

Throughout this book I am going to encourage you to pay more attention to your inner life. I am also going to show you step-by-step how to do that exactly the same way someone else showed me how to do it.

The first step is to establish a daily habit of prayer. If you can, stop by church in the morning or the evening, or at lunchtime. Try to establish a time each day to pray, and pray at the same time. Human beings thrive on routine.

I didn't realize it at the time (we rarely notice the most significant moments in our lives while they are actually happening), but the direction of my life changed that Sunday afternoon at the barbecue. John's invitation to spend ten minutes each day in prayer would shift the whole direction of my life. He would become a great spiritual mentor to me. He helped me to make sense of life. There have been many people in my life who have helped me grow spiritually, but he is more responsible than any other person for my spiritual development.

Ten minutes a day. What a simple concept. Try it for yourself. I know it will change your life just as it changed mine.

For twenty-five years I have been stopping by churches for ten minutes in dozens of countries and hundreds of cities. I love sitting in a quiet, empty church to pray. These days I am increasingly experiencing something that makes me very sad. I will be driving past a church and realize that I have a few minutes to stop in and get some advice from the guy with all the answers to every question. So I pull over, park the car, walk up the steps to the main entrance, and pull the door handle to go in, but it's locked. When most people need to go in and sit quietly in church with God, our churches are closed. We cannot schedule our crises according to the church's open hours. People cannot arrange their need for God between nine and five.

A man has an argument with his wife at ten thirty at night and leaves the house. Why is he going? He needs a little space, he needs to collect his thoughts, and he needs to think about what just happened. Where is he going? Probably to the bar, because that's the only place open at that time of night. If the local church were open he could go there. That's not to say that everyone would, but at least it would be an option. And he will be getting a very different perspective thinking about these things in the bar than he would praying about them in a church.

I have a dream that one day our churches will be open twenty-four hours a day. Imagine a world where every church is open all the time. The excuse we use is theft and vandalism. But if we were in our churches, these things wouldn't happen. If every Catholic spent ten minutes a day praying at their local parish church, our churches would be constantly teeming with life. The coming and going of hundreds of prayerful pilgrims would be enough to keep the vandals and thieves away.

As you begin to go deeper and deeper into prayer, God will help you to answer four questions: Who am I? What am I here for? What matters most? What matters least?

By developing clarity around these four questions you will become a phenomenal decision maker. You will no longer find yourself saying yes to things because you are afraid you will offend someone. Your yes will become a firm, passionate, mission-driven yes. And your no will become a firm, unwavering no.

"How is your prayer life?" Great spiritual directors have been asking those they guide this question for thousands of years. It is a little like going to the doctor and having your blood pressure taken first thing. This question allows us very quickly to get a sense of a person's spiritual health. Get into the habit of asking yourself the question and it will encourage you to continue to focus on the interior life.

The more you pay attention to your spiritual health, the more attuned you will be to your spiritual needs. When your body is hungry, your stomach growls. Your soul has ways of showing you it is hungry too. When I get impatient with my children or my colleagues, or a stranger, I know that my soul needs some attention.

Over time you will learn to listen to the cravings of your soul. Some days I crave silence. Other days my soul craves to serve others. There are times when you walk past the break room at work, catch a glimpse of a box of doughnuts, and immediately crave a doughnut. There are times when I catch a glimpse of a Bible and I have a craving to spend more time in the Scriptures. Before I ever started speaking and writing, I spent a lot of time sitting in empty churches reading, reflecting, praying. The ten minutes a day grew into longer and longer periods of time. The demands of my work and family life no longer allow me to spend such long periods of time in quiet, empty churches. But that was a wonderful season in my life, and I often crave that experience again.

When I think about this spiritual journey that I am sharing with you in these pages, I feel I have been fortunate beyond my wildest imaginings. Few things delight me more than sharing with you what God has freely given to me.

⭐ **KEY POINT**
God wants to bless you with spiritual vitality.

⚡ **ACTION STEP**
Establish a daily habit of prayer. Start with the Prayer Process, which you will find at the end of this book.

---

(10)

Get Busy Living

You are going to die. I know it's not a very uplifting idea, but it's true. You are going to die, and everyone you know is going to die. From the moment we are born, we are living with a death sentence. We don't know when we will die or how, but we do know we will die.

A couple of chapters back, I raised the question: When was the last time you paused to really think about your life? One of the most effective ways to do this is to pause and reflect upon death. This is why since the beginning of Christianity the Church has encouraged followers of Jesus to ponder the four last things: death, judgment, heaven, and hell. For a long time every parish would have a parish mission every year, and the topic would be the four last things.

If you went to the doctor next week and she told you, "You're very sick. You're dying. You only have six months to live," you would live the next six months very differently than you were planning to. That's why it is healthy for us to reflect upon death, because reflecting on the inevitability of it leads us to live our lives differently.

The reality of death rearranges our priorities. It may sound weird or warped, but I think being told by your doctors that you have six months to live is one of life's ultimate luxuries.

Most people get no warning. They are alive one minute and dead the next. But if your doctor tells you that you have three, six, or twelve months to live, you get the benefit of knowing that you need to get your affairs in order and the very great luxury of being able to say good-bye to those you love. Knowing that death is not far off brings remarkable clarity. After that news, there is no middle ground; something is either very important or not important at all.

A few years ago, I was doing some consulting work at a large hospital. The hospital was implementing the Dream Manager program for the nurses. The program helps people identify why they do what they do, what is important to them, and what their dreams are for the future. It has been incredibly successful in hundreds of companies, because sadly, most people have never been asked, "What are your dreams?" and most people spend more time planning their annual vacation than they spend planning their lives.

During the project I spent quite a bit of time with a group of hospice nurses. I remember wondering over and over again to myself, "How do they do it?" One day at lunch, I was sitting with five or six of them, and I asked them, "When people are dying, what do they talk about?" They told me that people who are dying very often talk to the nurses about how they wish they had lived their lives differently. Here is a sampling of what those nurses shared with me, twenty-four things dying people wished they had done differently.

- I wish I'd had the courage to just be myself.
- I wish I had spent more time with the people I love.
- I wish I had made spirituality more of a priority.
- I wish I hadn't spent so much time working.
- I wish I had discovered my purpose earlier.
- I wish I had learned to express my feelings more.
- I wish I hadn't spent so much time worrying about things that never happened.
- I wish I had taken more risks.
- I wish I had cared less about what other people thought.
- I wish I had realized earlier that happiness is a choice.
- I wish I had loved more.
- I wish I had taken better care of myself.
- I wish I had been a better spouse.
- I wish I had paid less attention to other people's expectations.
- I wish I had quit my job and found something I really enjoyed doing.
- I wish I had stayed in touch with old friends.
- I wish I had spoken my mind more.
- I wish I hadn't spent so much time chasing the wrong things.
- I wish I'd had more children.
- I wish I had touched more lives.
- I wish I had thought about life's big questions earlier.
- I wish I had traveled more.

• I wish I had lived more in the moment.
• I wish I had pursued more of my dreams.

These are the regrets of dying people, people who were out of time. Each of them contains a powerful lesson for those of us who are still living.

When I was in middle school I sang in the school choir. One of our duties was singing at funerals, and we sang at a lot of funerals. I remember thinking a lot about life and death as we sat there in church for all those funerals. Even at that age it struck me that life really is fleeting.

It is good and healthy to think about death from time to time. It puts things in perspective and reminds us what really matters. The perspective that death is inevitable reminds us to get busy living.

⭐ **KEY POINT**
It is healthy to reflect on the fact that life is short and we are all going to die.

⚡ **ACTION STEP**
If you died today, what would you wish you had done differently? Reflect.

11

Ordinary Things

I am a planner. Usually by June, my travel schedule for the following calendar year has been laid out, including personal travel. I am very organized. Everything has its place, and I like it when things are in their place.

Now, many people would see these as good qualities, but even our good qualities can get in the way of experiencing God. And it's amazing how our children pick up these things from us. On Sunday night when I am putting my six-year-old, Walter, to bed, he asks me, "What is the plan for this week, Daddy?" Then he likes me to go day by day through the whole week, laying out the schedule.

Planning is good and necessary up to a point, but we find God in the now. God lives in the eternal now. He is constantly inviting us to immerse ourselves in the present moment so we can be with him.

Sometimes planning the future can be a way of avoiding the present, and when we avoid the present we avoid God. Sometimes having everything in its place can be a way of trying to be in control, and sometimes it is a way of distracting ourselves from what really matters right now. Often we find God in the mess of our lives, the mess of our personalities, and the mess of our own brokenness.

One of the greatest mistakes in history has been to go off looking for God in the extraordinary. God occasionally uses the extraordinary to get our attention, but since the beginning his favorite place has been amid the very ordinary things of life. A child in a manger—what could be more ordinary?

A few years ago, when Dynamic Catholic was very young and we were growing very quickly, we spent a lot of time working out what the ideal team member looked like. After a year of discussions, we came to the conclusion that we were looking for three qualities. Each new candidate needed to be: committed, coachable, and aware.

This third quality, awareness, is one of the great gifts of the spiritual life. Most of the time we have awareness in hindsight. Most of us can look at something that happened last Christmas at a family gathering and say, "Now I understand what was really going on when Jim said that to Michael." This is awareness in hindsight. God wants to give you present-moment awareness. He wants you to be aware of things while they are actually happening. God wants you to be fully aware of every breath of air you take, every bite of food, every smile from a baby, every word you read, every song you hear, every kiss on the lips.

God loves ordinary things.

⭐ **KEY POINT**

God wants to give you present-moment awareness. He wants you to be aware of things while they are actually happening.

⚡ **ACTION STEP**

Learn to find God in the ordinary activities of daily life. At the end of the day, write down three times when you were fully aware of God in your day.

---

(12)

Living Soulfully

After the barbecue, John and I began speaking regularly. It was obvious that he had my best interests at heart. He was a friend of my soul, though I didn't realize it at the time. And that is a very difficult thing to find in this world, though I didn't realize that either.

He invited me to live soulfully. He awakened me in so many ways by reminding me that I was not just a body having a physical experience, but that I also had an eternal soul and that life is at least as much a spiritual experience as it is a physical one. He taught me to pay attention to spiritual things, and to recognize when my soul is hungry. Our stomachs growl when we are physically hungry. Our souls have a way of growling too. When we are spiritually hungry we become irritable, restless, and discontented.

Most people have an aha moment in their spiritual journey. I like to call it a Pentecost Moment. It is the experience that makes everything fall into place and make sense.

It doesn't mean we understand everything, but we go from not getting it to "Okay, I get it now!" From this point on we become more open to God, and more interested in things that are spiritual.

Some people have this Pentecost Moment while reading a book, others while attending an event or a pilgrimage, and still others on a weekend experience such as Christ Renews His Parish. Regardless of how and when this Pentecost Moment takes place, there is a before and after effect, just like there was with the disciples. Before Pentecost they were afraid and hiding; after Pentecost they went out with confidence to boldly proclaim Jesus' message to the world. In the same way, when we experience our Pentecost Moment the people around us can tell that something is different.

My own Pentecost Moment occurred with the discovery of a single idea, one of the great themes of Catholicism: the universal call to holiness, which is the concept that God calls every man and woman to the joy of a holy life. This idea captured my imagination in my late teens, causing me to take seriously the faith I had been baptized into as a child. It was the concept that made everything else fall into place for me. It was the central idea that connected the ordinary events of my life with the epic story of Catholicism.

This is what got my attention: Some things I do help me become the person God created me to be, and some things don't. It was as simple as that. It was practical, profound, logical, and life changing. Every moment is a chance to turn it all around.

By experimenting with this idea I quickly discovered that I was happier when I chose God's path. It was clear—there is a direct connection between happiness and holiness.

When I did something that I knew was God's will, something that would clearly help me become a-better-version-of-myself, I was filled with joy. When I did something that I knew was wrong or was clearly not good for me, that joy began to evaporate.

What also became quickly apparent to me was that you cannot stand still in the spiritual life. You can't take a break. That's like trying to stand still in the midst of a gushing river. You are either moving upstream or being pushed downstream—and only a dead fish floats downstream. And yet, moving upstream is not all about making a heroic effort to do spiritual things. It is as much about consciously making an effort to receive everything that God is pouring into you and learning to simply be with God.

Many years later I would come up with the phrase *the-best-version-of-yourself* to explain the universal call to holiness. I tried to speak to people about "the universal call to holiness," but their eyes would just glaze over. I kept experimenting with ways to say it that connected with people, and then one day while I was speaking, it just came out: "God wants you to become the-best-version-of-yourself." I knew instantly. I could tell by the audience's reaction. They got it. It made sense to them.

Every moment of every day, every situation, every person we encounter is an opportunity to become a-better-version-of-ourselves.

Going to Mass on Sunday, praying before meals, reading the Bible, sitting with a lonely friend and just listening, taking a few minutes to pray at the beginning of the day, reading a good spiritual book, going away on a retreat or pilgrimage, and serving the poor at a soup kitchen are all opportunities to grow in awareness and become a-better-version-of-ourselves.

When I first discovered these ideas as a teenager, they flooded me with energy and enthusiasm for life. I felt spiritually alive, and I was not going to trade that for anything. I looked each morning at the person I was and I knew I could be a better person, and I wanted to be better. The challenge was good for me. The world compares me to my neighbor, but God compares me to my former self. Every day God invites me to improve on my former self. It is a constant invitation to transformation.

The Pharisees focused on their belief that they were better than their fellow man. This type of thinking has infected every religion, organization, club, and association since the beginning of the world. Gather enough people together and there will be some who would rather focus on pretending they are better than others than concentrate on improving themselves.

I suppose we all go through a stage in life in which we compare ourselves to others. This is not a stage of great joy; it is a time of restlessness. We all fall into the trap of comparing ourselves with the person we think we should be. This doesn't lead to happiness either. It is a time of dissatisfaction. But if we are open to his grace, God will lead us to the-very-best-version-of-ourselves. This is a journey of a million steps, but in each step we find a happiness that is far beyond anything this world has to offer.

The true call of God is a call to personal conversion. Conversion is not a onetime experience. It is an ongoing journey. We take one step at a time. God is calling me to change. He is calling you to change. He invites me to change and grow every day, and he promises me his grace. He invites me not to become superior to other people, but to become superior to my former self. He wants my self of today to be a better self than my self of yesterday.

God invites me to collaborate with him in my daily conversion. But I am still resistant. I know the next step will bring as much if not more happiness than the last step he beckoned me to take, but I am resistant. I hope I can break through resistance today.

⭐ **KEY POINT**
Some things you do help you become the person God created you to be, and some things don't.

⚡ **ACTION STEP**
In each moment of each day choose the-very-best-version-of-yourself. Ask yourself, is what I am about to do going to help me become the-best-version-of-myself?

(13)

Hour by Hour

An hour of work might be the most ordinary thing in the world. In every town, village, suburb, and city around the world, billions of people are putting in an hour of work right now. It is a very ordinary thing, and God loves ordinary things.

Every day, ordinary people everywhere get up and go to work. Have you ever wondered why? Sure, the easy answer is to make a living, pay the bills, and support their families. This is good and noble, but is that really all there is to it? Okay, there are those people who get to do work they love—professional golfers, cancer researchers, rock stars. But what about the average person? Is there a higher meaning to his or her work?

In order to explore the meaning of work, we have to first ask ourselves about the purpose of work. What is its primary purpose? Making money? No. Making money is a secondary outcome of our work. The primary purpose of work is to help us become the-best-version-of-ourselves. When you work hard, pay attention to the details of your work, and do a good job, you grow in a number of virtues, including patience, diligence, perseverance, and integrity. Every time you grow in virtue, you become a-better-version-of-yourself.

Consider this example. Suppose you and I are neighbors, and there is a school at the end of the street. You live on one side of my house and Joe lives on the other side. One Thursday night I knock on Joe's door and say to him, "This Saturday they need some help planting trees at the school. Can you help?"

Joe says, "How much will you pay me?"

I say, "A thousand dollars an hour!"

"Great. I can help out for a couple of hours on Saturday, but not too early; I want to sleep in," Joe says.

On Saturday morning Joe comes down to the school at about eleven a.m., makes the rounds chatting to everyone, and then does a little work. But his work is sloppy. He doesn't work hard, he doesn't pay attention to the details, and he doesn't do a good job.

After a couple of hours Joe says he has to go, and he asks to be paid. He receives two thousand dollars for the two hours, but he does not go home fulfilled. The reason is because it is impossible to be fulfilled if you do a bad job.

The following Thursday night I knock on your door. You answer the door and I say, "This Saturday they need some help to finish planting those trees at the school. Can you help?"

"Sure, I'd be happy to volunteer," you say. "Let's get started early and we will get it finished before it gets too hot."

Saturday morning when I arrive you are already there and working hard. You work hard all morning, pay attention to the details, and do a great job. The trees look great. It is a real improvement. The school leaders are happy and grateful. When it's time to go home, I pat you on the back and say thank you.

You go home more fulfilled than Joe, even though you didn't get paid a single dollar.

The primary purpose of work is not to make money. Making money is a secondary outcome. Don't get me wrong—making money is good and necessary; it just isn't the primary purpose of our work. The primary purpose of work is to help us become the person God created us to be.

Hard work is good for us. It is part of God's plan for humanity. Even before Adam and Eve ate the apple and got evicted from the Garden of Eden, God gave Adam work to do. In Genesis 2:15 we read, "The Lord God took the man and put him in the Garden of Eden to work on the land and take care of it." Work isn't a punishment; it is part of God's purposeful plan.

One day I was complaining to John about having to study for an exam and he taught me a lesson that changed my life. He showed me how to transform an hour of work or study into an hour of prayer. This is possibly the most powerful spiritual lesson I have ever learned, because it is so everyday, every moment, practical. This is what he shared with me:

In Saint Paul's first letter to the Thessalonians he wrote, "Pray without ceasing" (1 Thessalonians 5:17). What do you think he meant? We cannot all go to church and pray all day long. And even if we could, we couldn't pray all day and all night—we need to sleep. But Paul said,

"Pray without ceasing." A machine operator needs to concentrate while he is operating the machine. He can't be praying and only half-paying attention to the machine. So what was Paul inviting us to?

As Christians we are called to transform every activity in our lives into a prayer. This is how we become the-best-version-of-ourselves and live holy lives.

John said to me, "When you study, take a pencil and write the initials of someone at the top of each page you read in your textbooks or at the top of each page of notes you write. Pause for a brief moment at the beginning of each page and offer the work on that page to God as a prayer for that person."

This is how we transform our work and study into prayer. And this is how our work and study transforms us into the person God created us to be.

Writing initials at the top of each page is perfect for a student, but perhaps it is not practical for your work. Another way to approach it is to offer each hour of your work to God as a prayer for a specific person or a particular intention. For example, you might offer the first hour of work each day for your spouse, and the second hour of work for your children. If you are not married, but feel called to be, you might offer the first hour of your work for your future spouse, wherever he or she is right now. You might offer the second hour of your work for your future children.

Pray for a friend who is sick, pray for your country, pray for people who have nobody to pray for them, pray for wisdom in a particular situation, pray for your parents, pray for your priest, pray for your parish . . . There are an unlimited number of people and situations to pray for by offering your work one hour at a time. In this way we bring unimaginable value to our work.

Some work has enormous intrinsic meaning, such as being a kindergarten teacher or working to cure cancer. Roles like these are filled with obvious meaning and value. But it is harder to see the meaning and value of selling widgets or serving burgers. When work is transformed into prayer, an hour of labor by someone who is serving burgers but offering it to God has more meaning and value than an hour by a brain surgeon who is only focused on how much money he will make for each surgery.

A trash collector can become a saint. Holiness isn't reserved for monks and nuns in monasteries and convents. A child can become a saint. It doesn't require age or education. Rich, poor, young, old, educated, uneducated, single, married—everyone is called to live a holy life. You are called to live a holy life. And your work—whatever it is—is one of the primary tools God has given you to grow in virtue, become the-best-version-of-yourself, and live a holy life.

Christianity is incredibly practical. It is a beautifully human invitation to experience the divine. For a Christian, everything is a prayer. Eating is a prayer. Sleeping is a prayer. Exercising is a prayer. Waiting is a prayer. Traveling is a prayer. Making love is a prayer. Working is a prayer. Resting is a prayer.

God loves ordinary things. The world is always trying to seduce us with the extraordinary. The culture fills our hearts and minds with spectacular dreams about hitting home runs, but life is about getting up every day and hitting a single.

Resistance hates ordinary, everyday action. Resistance likes to distract us, keep us thinking about things we can do nothing about.

Every man and every woman searches for meaning in their lives. As disciples of Jesus we are invited to bring meaning to everything we do. "You are the light of the world"; "You are the salt"; "You are the leaven in the bread." Jesus spoke all these words because he wanted our presence in the world to elevate and transform ordinary, everyday things. That's why he spoke about it using examples of ordinary, everyday things: light, salt, and bread.

By doing exactly the same things we did yesterday, but with a new mind-set, we are able to inject incredible meaning into the most mundane things—to take something as ordinary as washing the dishes and transform it into a conversation with God; to turn to God and pray an honest prayer: "Lord, I really don't feel like washing these dishes today, but I will do it and do it well. And I offer this task to you as a prayer for my friend Susan, who is suffering with cancer. Please ease her pain a little today. Amen."

Everything can be transformed into a prayer.

One of the hardest lessons to relearn in life is to be present. I say relearn because it would seem to me that as children we are very good at being present. But we lose that and then we have to learn it again. What's important now? Not what's important tomorrow or next week or next year, but what's important now. To give our full attention to whoever and whatever is before us right now. This is the wisdom of being present in the moment.

✪ KEY POINT

Every activity can be transformed into prayer.

⚡ ACTION STEP

Offer each hour or activity of your day to God as a prayer for a specific intention. Set an alarm to go off each hour. Take a deep breath and lift the coming hour up to God. Ten seconds at the beginning of each hour will change your life.

(14)

Interesting People

"If you want to be an interesting person, read books." This is what one of my high school teachers told us. At the time I didn't think too much about it, but time has proved him not only right but also wise.

The most interesting people I know are book readers. They love books. Many of the best conversations I have begin with "What are you reading at the moment?" There are so many good books in this world, and I don't have much time to read these days, so I find it fascinating to hear about what people are reading.

I must admit I didn't care much for reading before my spiritual awakening. You see, even today, I am a very slow reader. People don't believe me when I say it, and it is one of the reasons I am so passionate about audiobooks, because I read painfully slowly.

But I still remember as if it were yesterday the day John gave me an old Bible and suggested I read Matthew's Gospel.

"Have you ever read the Bible?" he asked.

"Not really," I replied. I remember I had one. It was a big, thick paperback version issued by the school. My mother had covered it with plastic to protect it, just as she did with all my schoolbooks. I remember lugging it to and from school in my school bag. I always had to have it at school for my religion classes, but I honestly don't remember ever opening it.

John handed me this old, worn Bible and something inside me warmed. It was as if someone had given me a treasure. You could just tell that this Bible had been read often. Looking back, I now know that not only had it been read, it had been prayed with. This Bible had been in the hands of someone holy. I didn't know if it had belonged to him or someone he knew, but it was mine now. I still have it. I know exactly where it is on the shelf in my study at home. It is an unforgettable part of my journey.

So, he gave me this Bible and challenged me to read the Gospel of Matthew in one sitting. He had no idea how slow a reader I was, so his challenge was a bit daunting to me. But I took the Bible, and a couple of days later I walked down to our parish church, which was maybe a mile and a half from our family home. I sat down in a pew and read Matthew's Gospel.

Every Sunday I went to church with my family, and every Sunday I heard a reading from one of the Gospels. But in some ways that is like seeing highlights from a movie each week and never seeing the whole movie. There is something very powerful about reading one of the Gospels from start to finish.

"What's next?" I asked John next time I saw him. He encouraged me to read the rest of the New Testament, one chapter a day. He also suggested I pick out the verse or phrase in each chapter that most stood out to me, and have a brief conversation with God about what the verse or phrase was saying to me.

I didn't realize it at the time, of course, but little by little, he was helping me to build a spiritual life.

Many years later, I was invited to do an off-site training for the executive team of a Fortune 500 company. As part of the preparation I asked the CEO and his team to print out the previous three weeks of their calendars to use in one of the exercises.

I was surprised to see that at seven o'clock every morning the CEO had an entry in his calendar that was simply labeled "Bible." I wasn't surprised that he read the Bible. I was surprised that it was on his schedule. The one thing I have learned in all the years I've been doing this exercise with corporate executives is that most people don't put the most important things on their schedules. People tend not to put exercise, prayer, spending time with their spouse and children, going to church, and many other important activities on their schedules. As a result these things often get neglected or pushed aside.

The most important things are almost never urgent. That's why it's essential that we schedule them.

"How long have you been taking time to read the Bible each morning?" I asked the CEO.

"About seven years," he replied.

"What happened seven years ago?"

"Great question," he said and laughed. "Seven years ago I became the senior vice president of sales in the middle of the biggest recession since the Great Depression." He paused for a long moment and then continued, "I just knew I needed help with the job."

"Do you do it every day?" I asked.

"No. I wish I could say I did, but I don't."

"Can you tell the difference between a day when you take the time to do it and a day when you don't?"

"Absolutely; it's like night and day. The thing is, I am happier when I do it. I am a better leader, a better husband, a better father, just a better person when I do it. But almost every day I feel a pull not to do it."

That's resistance. We experience it in every part of our lives in which we attempt anything that is good for us or worthwhile.

People who read the Bible regularly make better decisions. The Bible gives us incredible insight into the mind of God.

The Bible is full of interesting people. Some of them walked with God and some of them walked away from God, and most of them did a little bit of both. It is fascinating to watch the people in the Bible making decisions. So many decisions are based on fear and so few are based on faith. Do you make your decisions based on fear or on faith?

Have you just read a little bit of my story? Or have you just read a little bit of your story? That's entirely up to you. If you only read a little bit of my story, you will just keep on reading. But if you recognized something of yourself in my story, you will make plans to read Matthew's Gospel from start to finish in one sitting. Then begin the habit of reading one chapter of the Bible each day, picking out a verse or a phrase that strikes you and having a conversation with God about what those words are saying to you. And remember, if you don't schedule it, it probably won't happen.

Our lives change when our habits change. Resistance hates good, strong, positive habits in your life.

⊛ **KEY POINT**
People who regularly read the Bible make better decisions.

⚡ **ACTION STEP**
Set aside a few minutes each day to read and reflect on a passage from the Bible. Begin with Matthew, Proverbs, or Psalms.

Falling in Love

The day you fall in love with learning, your life changes forever. I went to fabulous schools growing up, but they didn't teach me to love learning. Throughout my teenage years I had a job after school at a pharmacy, riding my bike to deliver medications to the elderly. The pharmacist was a man named Brian Brouggy. He taught me to think. He was like a modern-day Socrates, raising questions for me to think about. If I said, "I don't know, tell me," he would say, "Think about it while you are riding around today and see what you come up with." When I came back he would ask me what I'd come up with. He wouldn't let up until I expressed my thoughts on the topic. Then he would make me defend what I said. He would challenge everything I said, even if he agreed with it.

My spiritual awakening ignited my love of learning. I suddenly went from being a kid who almost never finished an assigned book in school to being one who was not only reading everything for school but also reading great spiritual books on the side. I became very hungry to learn more about the faith. As I look back I still don't understand it. All I can say is that by some grace—and it really can only have been grace—I became fascinated, intrigued, and curious about everything to do with the Catholic faith.

When my eldest son, Walter, first went to school, his teacher asked me what my hopes were regarding his education. I told her what I will tell every teacher my children ever have: "I don't really care if he learns to read first in his class or last in his class; eventually he will learn to read. I want you to work with Meggie and me to instill in him a love for learning." If children develop a love for learning, they will become lifelong learners—and continuous learners tend to be successful at everything they turn their attention to.

Wherever you find excellence, you find continuous learning. They go hand in hand. Wherever you find that continuous learning is missing, you find mediocrity.

When you get close to the best of the best at anything, you always discover that they insanely persist at learning more about their craft. I have seen it in great actors and I have seen it in great golfers. I have seen it in musicians and painters, entrepreneurs and sailors, chefs and tech geniuses.

Whatever your age, if you have not yet fallen in love with learning, begin that love affair today. How? Go wherever your interests lead you. It is the perfect place to start. Rekindle a childlike curiosity. Ask why a lot. Free yourself from outcomes; you don't need a reason and you don't need to accomplish anything.

I love to read, but the commitments of life have made it more and more difficult to find time to do so over the past few years. So this year

I made it one of my resolutions. Each year I make New Year's resolutions, and usually I end up with a bit of a laundry list. Some of them I ultimately accomplish, and others I don't.

Each year in early December I make a trip home to Australia for a few days to visit my mother and my brothers, to reconnect with old friends, and to simply stay in touch with my roots and remember where I came from. I usually speak in the Los Angeles area on the Friday night and the Saturday morning, and then fly to Australia that Saturday night, landing in Sydney first thing Monday morning. This trip also provides a perfect opportunity to think about the year that is ending, and the year that is ahead.

As I boarded the plane last year I started thinking about what resolutions I would make for the New Year. The arrival of baby Ralph in August that year meant that we now had four children six years old and under. I have vague and distant memories of what it was like to be single. I remember going to movies more and going out to eat more. I remember a lot of things. In fact, I cannot remember the last time I went to the movies.

So as I thought about what to put on my list of resolutions for this year I decided to abandon the laundry list approach and focus on the four things that I knew would be the difference between just another year and a great year. This is what I came up with:

1. Pray every day.
2. Exercise every day.
3. Read every day.
4. Write every day.

If you had asked me when I wrote them which would be the hardest to fulfill, I would have said exercise without even blinking. But the hardest one to fulfill has been the reading. Now, don't get me wrong—resistance is always looking to block me from doing any of these. Resistance will do everything it can to prevent me from praying, exercising, reading, or writing. But for some reason I have really had to work very hard to carve out a few minutes to read each day this year. And there have been a lot of days when I have plain and simply failed.

It is one thing to fall in love, and it is something completely different to keep that love alive. This is true in both human love and our love for learning.

In my book *The Rhythm of Life* I wrote:

> In the room where I write in my home, I have more than a thousand books. But on the top shelf of one of the bookcases, at eye level, I have thirty-seven books. Each of those books has had an enormous impact on my life. I can tell you where I bought them, what city of the world I was in when I read them, and what the circumstances and situations of my life were at the time. There are books about philosophy, theology, psychology, business, and history. There are some incredible novels and biographies, and there on that shelf you will find some of the greatest spiritual and inspirational classics of all time. It is in a sense my own Great Books collection.

Over the years I have received thousands of requests for a list of the thirty-seven books. And while I have always freely shared a list of ten of these books, I have never published the whole list of thirty-seven. There are a few reasons, but let me share just a couple. First, about once a year I review the shelf, and usually a couple of books will come off and a couple of books will be added—new discoveries that out-shine what had a place on the shelf before. Second, this is in some ways the intellectual equivalent of asking to see me naked.

The reason I share this story with you is because I would like to en-courage you to build your own little shelf of books. It will be your own personal library of favorites. My shelf is filled with books that I could read over and over again, and many of them I do. But you can decide your own criteria for what you put on your shelf.

Great books feed us. They focus our minds and inspire our hearts. And great spiritual books help us to pray. John taught me never to go to prayer without a good spiritual book. Some days it is easy to engage in conversation with God, and other days we have trouble get-ting that conversation started. On those days, a good spiritual book can be a great help to our prayer. I was taught to read a paragraph or two and then talk to God about what I've read and what it means to me, how it comforts me or challenges me.

The other thing great spiritual books do is align our minds with the mind of God. There is so much confusion and negativity in the world. God wants our minds to be clear thinking and positive.

I am not naturally a very positive person. When I was younger it seems I was a lot more positive. But these days my mind does not at first instinct go toward the positive. Perhaps I have seen too much of the world, been disappointed by too many people, seen how cruel human beings can be to each other, and had my heart broken too many times, not just in love but in a dozen different ways.

Our culture is so cynical and skeptical, and it is easy to get sucked into that. All these reasons are why it is so important to align our minds with the mind of God. As Christians we are called to be people of possibility who are filled with hope. Positive thinking is a natural part of the Christian life. The phrase *positive thinking* was kidnapped and distorted in the later part of the twentieth century by people who tried to pretend that if they filled their minds with positive thoughts they would be able to accomplish anything. They disconnected the positive thinking from a hope we place in God. In fact they disconnected it from God altogether. The main difference is that as Christians we know that if we are separated from God we cannot do anything (John 15:5).

The Bible invites us over and over again not to be gloomy, not to lose ourselves in thoughts about worst-case scenarios, but to trust in God and to fill our hearts and minds with positive thoughts. Here are a few examples:

"This is the day the Lord has made, let us be glad and rejoice." (Psalm 118:24)

"Whatever is true, whatever is honorable, whatever is just, whatever is pure, whatever is pleasing, whatever is commendable, if there is any excellence and if there is anything worthy of praise, think about these things." (Philippians 4:8)

Whatever you ask for in prayer with faith, you will receive." (Matthew 21:22)

"I know the plans I have for you, says the Lord, plans for your welfare and not for harm, to give you a future with hope." (Jeremiah 29:11)

"Be transformed by the renewal of your mind." (Romans 12:2)

"Do not be anxious about anything." (Philippians 4:6)

"I can do all things through him who strengthens me." (Philippians 4:13)

"Put away from you all bitterness and wrath and anger and wrangling and slander, together with all malice, and be kind to one another." (Ephesians 4:31–32)

"Ask and you will receive; search, and you will find; knock, and the door will be opened for you." (Matthew 7:7)

"So we can confidently say, 'The Lord is my helper; I will not fear; what can man do to me?'" (Hebrews 13:5)

Fill your mind with thoughts of God. Spend your days thinking about things that are good and true and beautiful and noble, and you will become good and true and beautiful and noble.

It is clear that God does not want us to be negative thinkers. But he also doesn't want our thinking to be

neutral. He wants us to be positive thinkers on an epic scale.

So, I invite you to fall in love with learning again, or for the very first time. Become a continuous learner, especially in the area of your faith. God wants to transform your mind, and in doing so, he will turn you into an amazingly interesting person, so he can send you out into the world and lead more people to understand the genius of his ways.

⭐ **KEY POINT**
Wherever you find excellence, you find continuous learning. They go hand in hand. Wherever you find that continuous learning is missing, you find mediocrity.

⚡ **ACTION STEP**
Do something today to stoke your love of learning.

16

No Visitors

John and I started playing basketball. It gave us a chance to talk. That mostly turned out to be me asking him questions about things I had read. One thing that impresses me the most about him in hindsight is that if I asked him a question and he didn't know the answer, he would either tell me where I could find it and ask me about it the next week, or he would say to me, "Let me find out and I'll let you know." Then he did. So often when people say, "Let me get back to you," they never do, especially with questions about faith and spirituality.

Each week he would check in with me. He'd ask me about my spiritual habits, see how school and work were going, and just generally show an interest in me as a person.

"How's your ten minutes a day going?" John asked.

"Great."

"You doing it every day?"

"Most days."

"What about your Bible—you reading a chapter a day?"

"Yes."

"How about your study—are you turning each hour into a prayer for someone?"

"Yep, I'm doing pretty good with that. It helps me focus."

"Are you happier?" he asked.

I looked him in the eye and said, "Yes, thank you!"

"You're welcome. So, what are you doing on Saturday afternoon?" All of a sudden I got defensive. It was instinctive. I didn't know it at the time, but it was resistance.

"I'm busy Saturday afternoon," I lied.

"Busy doing what?" he asked, calling my bluff.

"Busy being busy," I joked, trying to deflect.

"Come on," he said. "Just give me two hours on Saturday afternoon."

This guy had changed my life. I mean, it was ultimately God, but John facilitated the introduction, and who knows where I would be if he hadn't played his role in God's plan? And besides all that, I was happy. I was happier than I had ever been in my life. I had clarity. I felt like for the first time in my life I had a really good sense of who I was and what really mattered. But still, I was resistant. I was resisting him. I was resisting happiness. I was resisting a-better-version-of-myself. I was re-sisting God. Even though every time I took the next step John invited me to take I was always glad I did, I still resisted every next step.

By now we were six or eight months into the process. Of course, I had no idea it was a process, but he had a beautiful plan. "I've only asked you to do three things," he said. "Have those things made you happier? Made you a better person? Helped you get close to God?"

"Absolutely," I replied.

"Then why are you so resistant?"

I just looked at him.

Since then I have seen resistance everywhere. I see it in myself, my wife, my children, my colleagues at work, my brothers, and my friends. I see it in the workplace and I see it in my parish. Understanding this resistance is essential to understanding people, how they live, why they do what they do, and why relationships are healthy or dysfunctional. It's essential to understanding ourselves.

"Come on. Give me two hours Saturday afternoon," he persisted. "I'll pick you up at your place at two o'clock." Reluctantly I agreed.

On Saturday he picked me up and we drove for about fifteen minutes to a neighboring suburb. "Where are we going?" I asked.

"You'll see."

He stopped in front of a nursing home. He opened the back door of the car and pulled a box of chocolates out of his briefcase. I was thinking we must be visiting someone he knew. We went into the nursing home and he walked up to the nurse's station and asked, "Is there anybody here who doesn't get many visitors?"

"Turn right here, walk down the hallway, go in any door and you will be in the right room."

Now, there's something you need to know about me. I'm an introvert. I know, I get up there and speak to all those thousands of people, but that is different. I'm at home up there, comfortable and relaxed. But put me in a small social gathering with twenty people I don't know, and I'd be quite happy standing in the corner people watching. So walking into a stranger's room in a nursing home wasn't in my comfort zone.

John walked up to the first door, knocked, waited to be invited in, went in, introduced himself, introduced me, and offered the gentleman, who was probably in his mid-seventies, a chocolate. The man invited us to sit down and he started talking to us as if he had been on a desert island for ten years and we were the first people he had seen since.

After about ten minutes, John got up, thanking the man for his time with a grace that reminded me of my father. My dad had this ability to do someone a favor and at the same time make the person feel like he or she was doing him a favor. I didn't realize it at the time, but this old man was doing me a favor.

We moved to the next room and did the same thing. John knocked, we went in, he introduced us, offered the elderly woman a chocolate, sat down, and simply talked to her.

This was my first intense encounter with loneliness. I had seen a kid at school sitting alone at lunchtime. I had been the kid sitting alone at lunchtime. But this was different. This was a profoundly sad loneliness that seemed unnecessary and on some level inhumane. Little did I know that in the coming decade I would develop a very intimate relationship with loneliness myself.

I published my first book when I was nineteen, and started speaking and traveling a few months later at twenty. When I sit down and think about my twenties, I find it very difficult to remember things in a cohesive or chronological way. During that decade I averaged more than 250 days each year on the road. People joke about it, but I would literally wake up and not know where I was. It wasn't until late in that decade that I settled in the United States, so for most of it I was caught between two continents, moving back and forth between Australia and America.

I was lonely, disconnected, and rootless, but I didn't realize it. The momentum of my life and the excitement of it all had lifted me from the ground and was carrying me along like a potato chip bag in a strong wind. Only when some normalcy entered my life did I realize how very unhealthy all that traveling can be. Life on the road is not natural. It is a rootless experience. The nomadic life wasn't for me.

It wasn't until many years later when I was married that I realized how desperately lonely I was during those years. I remember waking up one morning about a week after Meggie and I got back from our honeymoon. I walked into the kitchen and sat down. We had breakfast together and had the most ordinary conversation. But I remember thinking to myself, "Wow, this is really fabulous."

Being alone is not the same as feeling lonely, but one can slip effortlessly into the other without a moment's notice. Perhaps this is why people obsess about ensuring they always have plans and always have someone around.

The fear of being alone is the father of many relationships that never should have been. When we choose to be with someone because we are afraid of being alone, we dishonor ourselves and the other person.

The loneliness, of course, served a purpose. It is a great teacher. It's a form of pain, and pain can be a ruthless teacher. You put your hand on a hot stove and you learn not to do that again, but that can be a brutal lesson. Loneliness is not brutal like that, but it can be a painful way to learn. Interestingly, solitude is the cure for loneliness. When we are afraid of being alone, we should go into it. Dive deep into it. Solitude teaches profound lessons, especially about ourselves. Feeling lonely has value. Sometimes we need to turn inward to discover what we need to hold on to and what we need to let go of.

One of life's most essential lessons is learning to be alone.

In many ways, I believe that until we learn to be comfortable alone—and more than that, to enjoy our own company—we are not really ready to live a bold and passionate life. And until we learn this lesson we are unconditionally unprepared to be in any kind of significant relationship with another person.

A thirty-year-old woman is more comfortable saying no when a man asks her out on a date. Her twenty-two-year-old self might have said yes. But she knows herself better now. And she knows that a hot bath, a good book, and a nice glass of wine are better than some dates. She has learned to be comfortable in her own company. It is an invaluable lesson.

Until we really know ourselves, we waver a lot, and come down on the wrong side of too many decisions. Once we get to know ourselves and establish a sense of self, we find ourselves in possession of a rare clarity that teaches us that if it is not a definite yes, it is a definite no.

Loneliness, or solitude, or perhaps both, teach us who we are deep down beyond the influences of parents, teachers, friends, and current culture. Loneliness and solitude teach us what is really important and what is trivial nonsense. Loneliness is a form of hunger, and hunger is good for us. Loneliness and solitude teach us gratitude. Yes, there are differences between the two, but they intermingle and often it is impossible to separate them.

These elderly men and women in the nursing home were intensely lonely in many cases, and they didn't have a lot of tomorrows to look forward to. Every single one of them had a story to tell about their lives, and those stories were filled with fabulous lessons about life, love, work, success, failure, marriage, parenting, hopes and dreams, fears and regrets. But they had nobody to tell their stories to.

John and I went from room to room for two hours. At the time I was about sixteen years old, and toward the end of each of these short visits, John would ask the person, "What were you doing when you were sixteen?" After listening to each person's answer, he would point to me and say, "This young man is sixteen years old—what advice do you have for him?"

Answering that single question revealed their hopes, dreams, values, and regrets. It was an education in itself. A thousand times since then I have wished I had recorded their answers.

I spent many Saturday afternoons at that nursing home and others in the area. At first I would always go with John, but after a few months I started going on my own. I even tried to take some of my friends from high school. They just thought I was crazy. In all honesty, I don't know why I went as often as I did. I didn't like going. I never got comfortable with it, but I suppose somewhere deep inside I knew it was good for them and good for me. And there was no mistaking the fact that each time I walked in the door I was making their day.

I suppose we all need a chance to get outside ourselves and serve other people. It seems the earlier in life we get this chance in a real and tangible way—a chance to serve others, know that we have worth, discover our innate ability to make a difference in other people's lives—the better off we are.

⭐ **KEY POINT**

We keep resisting God even after we are convinced that his way is the best way.

⚡ **ACTION STEP**

Visit the lonely. Somewhere not too far from where you live, someone is saying a prayer. He is asking God to send someone to visit him and lift him up out of the depths of his loneliness. God wants you to help him answer that prayer.

An Unconventional Education

Years later, when I first began speaking and writing, people would ask me, "You are so young—how do you know about all these things?"

I've had an unconventional education. The older I get, the more I realize that life teaches us all the lessons we need to learn to take the next step in our lives and to fulfill our mission in life. It is easy to focus on the formal aspects of our education, but the informal aspects are often the most influential.

For starters, growing up in a large family taught me a lot about life. Then there were the great schools, afternoons at the pharmacy, great books, wonderful parents and siblings. But there are two factors that I always come back to. First, beginning in my late teens I spent a lot of time in the classroom of silence, sitting with God in empty, quiet churches. And I continue to believe that we can learn more in an hour of silence than we can in a year from books. And finally, speaking and writing gave me the opportunity to travel to more than fifty countries in my early twenties. This is an important time in anyone's life. It was fascinating to visit all those countries, seeing how different people live, experiencing the Church in so many countries and cultures, observing people in their daily lives and seeing what their struggles and priorities are.

It wasn't something I set out to do. I didn't plan to be an author, and I certainly didn't plan for public speaking to play a major role in my life. It just sort of happened. If I'd had things my way I probably would have become a marketing executive for Coca-Cola. Looking back now it is all clear, but at the time looking forward, the path ahead was misty and I could barely see a couple of steps ahead of me. So I just kept taking the next step, trusting in God. It was clear that he was involved. You simply couldn't have made that happen if a hundred people had dedicated themselves to it full-time.

Each step I took, at each stop along the way, I learned something that I needed to know somewhere else down the road. I was constantly being educated for the next phase of this mission. My worldview was constantly being challenged and expanded. The petty things I thought about or worried about were shown for what they were, in stark contrast to the real problems so many people face every morning when they wake up. And of course, all these experiences prepared me to write.

It's relatively easy to write about what is important to one person or some people, but I think to write something that is enduring, something that reaches the masses, you have to touch on universal themes. It's like trying to find a thick vein of gold running through a mine. What matters to everyone? What is everyone struggling with? All the travel and meeting so many different people gave me that. They would chat with me after my events, they would write letters to me, and I began to recognize these universal themes. This allowed me to continually hone the message. I didn't set out to be a writer, but for a writer this is a beautiful gift.

It was also fascinating from a spiritual perspective. People tend to have a very local experience of their faith, which is usually tied fairly closely to their parish. On one level this is very good and necessary. The parish is the lifeblood of the Catholic experience in many ways. But we're human beings, so there is a tendency toward self-interest, and in this context there is always the danger that a parish will turn in on itself and become more like a country club than a mission-driven community reaching out to share the love of God with others.

What's the biggest thing happening in your parish this year? Or, what is the biggest challenge your parish is facing at the moment? Or what are people in your parish disagreeing about right now?

When you take these questions and drop them into a parish in Honduras, Guatemala, or Tanzania, there's a pretty good chance that putting them in this context is going to make them look a little ridiculous. Context is powerful. And sure, these might be extreme examples, but if you take the answers to these questions for the average suburban parish in the United States and apply them to the average parish in Italy, Portugal, or even Ireland—countries that have been Catholic at the core for centuries—there is a pretty good chance that in those places they wish they had your problems. Or take your issues and drop them into the average inner-city parish right here in the U.S., and they would consider your challenges to be high-class problems.

One man's trash is another man's treasure. And that is true not only of things but also of experiences and problems.

By the time I was in my mid twenties I had seen more of the world than most presidents and bishops. I don't say this in a boastful way, but I think it is an important part of my journey, and a fact that helps some of the other pieces fall into place. Experiencing the Church in so many different countries and cultures gave me a unique perspective of what Catholics were grappling with at that time in history. It allowed me to work out what was local and what was universal, what was unique to one group of people and what was common to people everywhere.

Whether it was spending those Saturday afternoons in the nursing homes, reading great books, or traveling the world, these things gave me a fundamental education about people. Being in those nursing homes helped me to see a whole life. Multiple generations of people used to live together in families, but the mobility and disintegration of families in the modern age has us too often living in our own little bubbles. For a teenager, in particular, that is very dangerous. The things we think are monumentally important when we are teenagers really are quite sad and embarrassing when you step back. But there in those nursing homes, the elderly men and women would reveal their whole lives to me—the ups and downs, the triumphs and tragedies— and I got to see how life really unfolds. This is one of the reasons I love reading biographies and autobiographies. When you read about a person's whole life—the good, the bad, and the ugly—it allows you to put the situations of your own life into perspective. Otherwise we have a tendency to isolate and dwell on particular situations rather than seeing our lives as a whole.

For most people their priorities get rearranged, usually for the better, as they get closer to death. We spoke about the four last things, and they are very much on people's minds in an environment such as a nursing home. They are no longer abstract questions; they are real and near. It was a very stark lesson to me that we are all just passing through this world, and no matter what lengths we go to to make ourselves comfortable, this is not home.

It was an amazing thing to see God work through me. It was a small thing, spending time in the nursing home. It was so ordinary and so simple to just sit and talk with someone for a few minutes. But there was grace there, and even in my spiritual and worldly immaturity, I was still able to recognize that God was at work. And once you get a taste of God working through you to bring joy to others, you are hooked. There is no better feeling in the world.

A few short years later I would be in need of mercy myself. Setting off at twenty years old to speak and travel, I was almost entirely at the mercy of those who opened their hearts and their homes to me. I remember my mother was very worried. She worried for a long time. Come to think of it, I believe she still worries a bit when I am traveling. But people have been so good to me. For twenty-five years they have been welcoming me. I have been a stranger to them and they have been strangers to me, but they have loved and welcomed me like I was their own child. Anytime I pause to reflect upon it, my eyes begin to well with tears. It is astonishing to me how much complete strangers have loved me. I don't understand it. I cannot explain it. But it has always filled me with tremendous gratitude.

Loneliness is one of the great evils of our age.

Somewhere not too far from where you live, someone is saying a prayer. He is asking God to send someone to visit him and lift him up out of the depths of his loneliness. His wife may have passed away and his children may live in other cities. Or maybe they just neglect him. It may be a neighbor down the street, it may be an old friend, or it may be a complete stranger whom the Holy Spirit points out to you today. Whatever the case, this person is praying to God and asking him to take away the wicked sting of loneliness.

God wants you to help him answer that prayer. Visit the lonely. It takes only a few minutes. Make this a habit. It will bring you unimaginable joy and a deep, deep satisfaction.

⭐ **KEY POINT**
Life is always teaching us lessons.

⚡ **ACTION STEP**
What lesson is God trying to teach you through the experiences of your life at the moment? Reflect.

---

(18) Tuesday Nights

John and I were talking one day and as usual he asked me how my daily prayer was going, and if I had any questions about what I was reading in the Bible. These were regular conversations, but from time to time I got the sense that he was getting ready to lead me to a new place, to introduce a new habit, and resistance would rise up in me. I would get defensive. My physical demeanor would tighten. I am sure my body language was horrible. Nonetheless, with my very best interests at heart, he pressed on.

"I've got something else for you," John said, smiling.

"Really?"

"Yep. I think it's time for you to really discover the Mass."

"Well, I already go to Mass every Sunday," I said.

"Great, but that's not what I'm talking about."

"What are you talking about?"

"Daily Mass."

"You're crazy—there is no way I can go to Mass every day."

"That's not what I had in mind. I was thinking maybe just one day each week."

"Why?" I asked him.

"It's different. There is something very powerful about a small group of people gathering for the Eucharist."

Needless to say I was resistant. When I wrote at the beginning that I have been resisting God and resisting happiness my whole life, I meant it. It wasn't just words. I resist and then I surrender. I resist and then I surrender. The surrender comes because I see the stupidity of resisting or because resisting gets to be miserable, or through grace.

I have used that word a few times in this book, and we use it a lot at church. But I suspect if every reader defined grace, no two definitions would be the same. What is this grace I speak of? Grace is the help God gives us to respond to his call, and to do what is good and right. We do nothing to deserve this gift of grace, and yet, as a loving father lavishes gifts upon his child, God lavishes grace upon us. In the context of our topic, grace gives us the strength to break through resistance so that we can do things that are healthy and worthwhile. It may be as simple as going for a run or sitting down to pray, or it may be something much larger, such as agreeing to serve as a missionary for a year or getting married.

The point is, I was once again resistant to John's suggestions. As usual, it took me a few days to warm to this idea. The following Sunday I picked up a copy of the parish bulletin to see what time Mass was each day. Six forty-five a.m. Ouch! I'm not really a morning person. I like to stay up late, working deep into the night. It is not uncommon for me to go to bed at three or four a.m. Then, I noticed in tiny print at the bottom of the Mass schedule that in addition to the morning Mass on Tuesdays there was a Mass in the evening at seven thirty—perfect for me.

So I started going to Mass on Tuesday evenings. My family and I belonged to a fairly large parish in Strathfield, a suburb of Sydney. On Sundays the church was full and bustling with lots of young families. But come Tuesday night it was quiet, just the priest and me and about eleven or twelve others.

I didn't get the Mass until I started to going during the week. There is something about the intimacy of those daily Masses that creates a different experience. It is the same Mass, but you hear things in a different ways; you witness things in a different way. The prayers of the Mass are both ancient and fresh. They speak of yesterday and apply to your life and mine today. I fell in love with the Mass during weekday Masses, because it was there in those intimate experiences that I really started to understand it.

Once you understand that God has an incredible dream for you, once you grasp that he wants you to become the-best-version-of-yourself and help others to do the same, and once you start to listen to the prayers of the Mass with all this in mind, you very quickly discover that there is genius in Catholicism.

The other thing I found very powerful about weekday Mass was the homily. Our priest would give, literally, a one-minute homily. One minute, but it was always spot on. It gave you just enough to chew on, just enough to work on.

Those first few weekday Masses are beautiful memories in my spiritual journey. I can never re-create those first experiences, but I find myself longing for them. Over these many years on the road, occasionally a priest will offer to say a private Mass for me and the team. Those are always special moments.

Little by little John was helping me to develop a vibrant inner life. No doubt someone had done the same for him and he was now passing it along to me. Or perhaps he developed his own interior life by trial and error, and wanted to save me the heartache. Either way I was grateful. I was grateful then and with every passing year my gratitude has grown.

⭐ **KEY POINT**

Once you understand that God has an incredible dream for you, once you grasp that God wants you to become the-best-version-of-yourself and help others to do the same, and once you start to listen to the prayers of the Mass with all this in mind, you very quickly discover that there is genius in Catholicism.

⚡ **ACTION STEP**

Go to Mass twice this week, Sunday and any other day you like. Pay attention to how it focuses you and fills you with peace.

---

(19)

Bored?

Growing up, my brothers and I knew there were certain things you just didn't say. One of those was "Shut up!" If we told someone to shut up, Mom or Dad would be on us in an instant. Another forbidden phrase was "I'm bored!" This would especially drive my father crazy. He grew up in London in the kind of poverty most people only ever read about. He started working when he was twelve years old, and kept working hard his whole life. I am sure he looked at our lives as children, and all the things and opportunities we had, and wondered how his life might have been different if he'd had the same opportunities.

To say we are bored at any moment in our lives is a massive insult to God, but to say we are bored at Mass takes the insult to whole other level.

Each Sunday morning my brothers and I would hold an election to figure out who would talk to our father and ask him if we had to go to church. We knew the answer, because we had attended the ten a.m. Mass at Saint Martha's Church every Sunday of our lives. But we would pull out the greatest hits and try our best. We were either slow learners or extremely persistent. This is just one example of how the conversation would go:

Child: "Dad, do we have to go to Mass today?"

Dad: "No."

Child: "You're joking, aren't you?"

Dad: "No."

Child: "But there's more to it, isn't there?"

Dad: "Yes."

Child: "What?"

Dad: "You don't have to go to Mass if you can tell me the one thing that you are going to do while I am at church with all your brothers that is more important than going to church and thanking God for another week of life."

Child: "Um . . ."

Dad: "Okay. It might take a while to think about that, so while you are thinking about it, go and get dressed for church."

We walked to church every Sunday. When we arrived, Dad led us to the front row on the left-hand side. We sat there every Sunday. Never did we find someone else sitting in our seats. I've thought about that as I have gotten older, and I guess people in the parish just knew that was where we sat (not that people are generally fighting over the front row at church). Did we behave? I honestly don't know. I am sure we embarrassed our parents on many occasions.

Have you ever been bored at Mass? Sure, we all have. For decades parents and grandparents have been listening to kids say, "Do we have to go to Mass? It's boring." Today, it seems more and more adults are saying the same thing.

This is one of the biggest problems facing the Catholic Church at this moment in history. If we don't fix it, we are finished. Catholicism will be reduced to a small cultural curiosity if something is not done about this singular issue. You cannot have an increasing number of people believing that the central experience of Catholicism is boring and at the same time expect the future to be bigger than the past.

But what would you say if I could give you a game changer that would guarantee you would never again be bored at Mass, unless you wanted to be? Even more than that, this simple technique will transform your Sunday Mass experience into a source of practical wisdom to direct your life. Let's take a look at it together.

Boredom is a manifestation of selfishness. It can only occur when we are overly focused on ourselves. It always means that we have set God and neighbor aside to focus exclusively on ourselves, and that is never a recipe for happiness.

⊛ **KEY POINT**
To say we are bored at any moment in our lives is a massive insult to God.

⊛ **ACTION STEP**
If you are ever bored, look for a way to get outside yourself and serve others.

---

(20) Learning to Listen

The hardest lessons to learn in life are the ones we think we have already learned. Most people think they are good listeners, most people think they are good drivers, and most people think they are pretty good Christians. But compared to what?

In reality, most people are not as good as they think they are at these things. The false perception is the result of illusory superiority. This is cognitive bias, whereby individuals overestimate their own qualities and abilities relative to others.

From time to time it is good for us all to learn to listen again. Listen to those you love. Listen to your body. Listen to your conscience and soul. Listen to God.

One of the fastest ways to improve any relationship is to become a better listener. There are dozens of ways to do this. Let's take a look at a few together.

- Look at whoever is speaking. Smile, make appropriate eye contact, and look at the person speaking. If you are not looking at that person you immediately signal, "I'm not interested"; "I'm not paying attention"; "I'm bored with you."
- Listen with your body. Your body language says a lot about how open or closed, interested or uninterested you are in what a person is saying. Be mindful of your body language and get yourself into a comfortable open position that makes it easier for you to listen. Pay attention to the other person's body language too. He may be telling you things with his body language that he is not telling you with his words.
- Don't interrupt. I don't know anyone who likes being interrupted. It signals, "What I am about to say is more important than what you were saying." If you disagree, wait your turn. Interrupting is broadly considered rude.
- Avoid distractions and disruptions. Be present to who is in front of you right now. Try not to be thinking about the next thing you are going to say; this tends to cause our minds to wander and we stop listening to whoever is speaking. Turn your phone to silent, or turn it off if possible. If that is not possible, at least explain to the person, "I'm sorry, I cannot turn my phone off for our conversation because I am expecting a really important call/text that is out of my control." Even if you are speaking to someone on the phone, most people can tell when you are multitasking. Even if a person cannot see you, she can sense if you are really listening to her.

- Ask questions. Nothing shows that we are engaged and interested like good questions. It is one of the key principles of active listening.
- Make sure you understand what the person is saying. If you are not sure, or if you think you are sure, it can be helpful to say, "What I am hearing you say is . . ." or "It sounds like what you're saying is . . ." This is another powerful tool for active listening, which, again, signals that you are trying hard to understand what the person is saying.

Everyone loves being listened to. There are a great many people in this world who feel like nobody ever really listens to them; as a result they also feel that nobody really understands them. They feel misunderstood even by those who are closest to them.

There is a beautiful verse in the book of Sirach that reads, "Conduct your affairs with humility, and you will be loved more than a giver of gifts" (3:17). Everyone loves receiving gifts, and we attach a certain affection to those who give us great gifts. To listen well, actively, and deeply requires humility. And in addition to the verse from Sirach, I think we can say, "Become a great listener and you will be loved more than a giver of great gifts."

Every relationship improves when we really start to listen, especially our relationship with God.

Too often we approach Sunday Mass with a passive disposition. It is perhaps the result of a culture that prefers us to be passive. The passive me says: "Feed me"; "Entertain me"; "Hold me"; "Love me"; "Listen to me"; "Tell me I matter"; "Make me a priority"; "Don't make me think too much or work too hard"; and so on. The passive self tends to be a very selfish self, and resistance loves the passive self. Resistance hates when you get into a proactive disposition. That is when resistance pulls out all its tricks, because it hates action.

If we wish to have a radically different experience at Mass on Sunday, the answer is not better music, better homilies, or a more welcoming community—though I am all in favor of these and agree we need to improve them. The key to transforming our Sunday Mass experience and improving our relationship with God is shifting from a passive to an active disposition and really listening.

Do you merely attend Mass or do you participate in Mass? The difference between the passive and the active approach is night and day.

Now for the game changer. This small habit alone will help you make a huge shift from passive to active.

One thing I have noticed about continuous learners is they tend to have pen and paper with them at all times, because they never know when they are going to hear something great or have an idea. For many years I have slept with a pen and paper beside my bed, as I often wake in the middle of the night with an idea and I am afraid I will forget it. This allows me to write the idea down and go back to sleep.

As Catholics we tend not to be continuous learners. One of the most striking examples of this is that you almost never see anyone in Church with pen and paper. It may seem small, but it says two things that are worth considering. First, when we come to church without pen and paper, we are indirectly saying, "Father is not going to say anything worth writing down." We have decided even before leaving home that this is the case. The second thing we are saying is, "God isn't going to speak to me at church today." But he does. He has been speaking to you, he is speaking to you, and he will continue to speak to you.

Here is the idea. Get yourself a small notepad, pocket size. This will be your Mass Journal. Visit DynamicCatholic.com and request a free one if you wish, but any small notebook will suffice. Bring it to Mass with you next Sunday. As you walk into church, greet God and ask him, "God, show me one way in this Mass I can become a-better-version-of-myself this week." Then listen.

Listen to the music, listen to the readings, listen to the preaching, listen to the prayers, and listen to the quiet of your heart. One thought or idea, one challenge or invitation will jump out at you. Write it down. Just one thing. Not five things, not sixteen pages of scribbling notes. Just the one thing. Write it down on its own page, and date it. Then spend the rest of Mass praying about how you can live out that one idea in the coming week.

You will go home from Mass focused, energized, and invigorated. Why? That's what happens when we listen to the voice of God in our lives. We get focused, energized, and invigorated. And if we are not focused, energized, and invigorated, it is usually a fairly good indication that we are not taking time to listen to the voice of God in our lives, that we are ignoring him and are instead off doing whatever it is we want to do.

I have been keeping a Mass Journal for nineteen years now. In my study at home, where I write, I have a whole shelf full of them. Sometimes, when resistance gets the better of me in the form of writer's block, I get up, walk over to that shelf, and take one of those small

Mass journals off the shelf. Perhaps I take the one from 2005 and spend a few minutes flipping through it, reading the things that God said to me that year.

Every time I do this, no matter which journal I choose from the shelf, I realize three things. First, there were things happening in my life back then that I thought were a big deal. They weren't. I was making a big deal out of nothing. Next, there were things I was really struggling with back then that I am no longer struggling with. God's grace has come into that part of my life and liberated me. Finally, there were things that I was really struggling with in 2005 and I am still struggling with them in 2016.

If I asked you what happened in your life in 2005, you could probably tell me you got married, had a baby, moved to a new city, bought a new home, started a business, got your fist job, or sent your youngest child off to college. But if I asked you what happened deep in your heart and soul in 2005, you probably couldn't tell me. Not because you have a bad memory or weren't paying attention, but because life carries us along and we lose track of the things happening deep within us.

Looking back at your Mass Journal(s) will become very enlightening over time. It will help you to recognize patterns in your life. It will help you see how persistent some of your struggles are. And it will help you to see how God helps you, leads you, challenges you, and encourages you. When we remember how God has been there for us in the past, we become confident that he will be there for us in the future.

It is impossible to be bored at Mass if you come to listen to what God has to say to you right now in your life. It doesn't matter how good or bad the homily is; God will speak to you through it. It doesn't matter how good or bad the music is; God will speak to you through it. Whether it is a wonderful, prayerful mood or there are kids running up and down the aisle throwing crayons and eating potato chips, God will speak to you.

Through the brokenness of the world, the imperfection of other people and situations, and even our own limited humanity, God wishes to speak to us. His thoughts and words will encourage and challenge us, guide and warn us, inspire and energize us.

Nothing will have more impact on your life and your experience of Sunday Mass than opening yourself up to what God wishes to say to you.

Now let's take the game changer beyond you personally. Imagine if everyone in your parish—even the children—came to Mass each Sunday with a Mass Journal, ready to listen to God's instructions for the coming week. I have seen this work with children as young as five and six years old. If a real and consistent effort were made to ingrain this as a habit in a parish, I have no doubt that it would have unbelievable impact. It would be the trigger. Thousands of other things would happen as a result of this simple new habit, but it would be the trigger. This initiative in a parish would ignite unmatched engagement. People would grow exponentially spiritually, and would hurry themselves to be more involved in the life of the parish.

People are bored at Mass. We have known this for fifty years. What are we doing? In most cases the answer is nothing or hoping it will change. Hope is not a strategy. In some cases, what we are doing is so vague and disconnected from the average Catholic's Sunday experience that it is making little difference.

I am no prophet, but I know this and will repeat what I said earlier: Boredom at Mass is one of the biggest problems facing the Catholic

Church at this moment in history. If we don't fix it, we are finished. Catholicism will be reduced to a small cultural curiosity if something is not done about this singular issue of people feeling bored at Mass. You cannot have an increasing number of people believing that the central experience of Catholicism is boring and at the same time expect the future to be vibrant and life giving.

Get yourself a little Mass Journal. I promise you, it will transform your experience of Mass. Encourage your children and friends to do the same. Consider starting an initiative in your parish to get everyone a Mass Journal, and teach them how to use it. We would love to partner with you at Dynamic Catholic to pilot that idea in your parish and help make it happen.

If we had complete awareness of what was really going on at that altar, we would crave the Mass. Believe it or not, there will come a time, in this life or the next, when you will be beyond happy, ecstatically joyful, all the time; a time when you will be completely content to go to Mass and do nothing else.

Let me give a couple more practical suggestions to improve your love, understanding, and awareness of the Mass.

When Mozart was a child, his father used to make him copy out the scores of great musicians such as Bach and Eberlin. Mozart would sit there for hours and hours, copying every single note for symphonies, operas, concertos, etc.

There is something about writing things down that increases our knowledge and retention. Write out the Mass. That's right. Get yourself a missal and write out the Mass word for word. You will be amazed how this simple exercise will increase your understanding and appreciation of the Mass.

The other exercise that you may find very powerful is to take a few minutes on Wednesday or Thursday each week and write out the Gospel reading for the following Sunday. You will be amazed how this increases your engagement with that reading. If you have children, invite them to write out the Gospel reading for next Sunday's Mass. It is a fabulous activity to do together each week. It will lead to wonderful conversations about the reading, and at Mass your children will be much more engaged.

The Mass is not boring, but we need to teach people how to appreciate it. It's time to put an end to people being bored at Mass.

⊛ **KEY POINT**
The most practical way to improve all our relationships is to continually become a better listener.

⚡ **ACTION STEP**
Make a conscious effort to listen to God and the people in your life.

The Power of Habits

Habits have a massive impact on our lives. For better or for worse, they can shape our destiny.

Resistance loves the negative patterns in your life, the bad habits. The path of least resistance effortlessly creates negative routines, rituals, and rhythms. Do you know what the negative patterns are in your life? Do you procrastinate by watching television? Do you try to spend your way to happiness? Do you eat when you are not hungry to deal with emotions? Do you drink to escape? Do you constantly check your e-mail or social media to avoid doing the most important things? Do you keep spending time with people even though you know they are not helping you become the-best-version-of-yourself?

We also have negative habits of the mind. Do you worry about things that you have no control over? Do you obsess about the worst possible outcome in situations? Are you constantly judging yourself and others? Do you keep returning to feelings of guilt even after God has forgiven you? Do you dwell on things in the past you wish you had done differently? Do you blame yourself even when something is not your fault? Do you doubt yourself constantly?

We all have routines, rituals, and rhythms that are negative. They have power over us. They have central places in our story. They stop us from becoming the-best-version-of-ourselves. These negative patterns are so easy to fall into.

Everything bad is a distortion of something good. Routines, rituals, and rhythms are a powerful force for good in our lives. They are central to creation, and therefore part of God's ingenious plan for you and me.

What are the positive patterns in your life? They may be simple and seemingly insignificant, but they glue your life together in a profoundly positive way. It could be driving your kids to school, reading the newspaper in your pajamas on Saturday, what you eat for breakfast, walking the dog, making love to your spouse, or reading before you go to bed. Each of these is an informal routine or ritual. They create powerful rhythms in our lives, and together these routines, rituals, and rhythms hold our lives together in ways we will probably never understand.

But let me ask you a question: When was the last time you set out intentionally to create a life-changing habit? Overcoming resistance is hard to do a hundred times a day. We get hungry, angry, lonely, tired, and we end up giving in. That's where habits come in.

My whole life I have been studying champions and excellence. I have been fascinated with the best of the best at anything. The one observation I have continually made over the years is that the best of the best—the enduring sports figures, the business leaders, the saints—have better habits.

Habits effortlessly defeat resistance. The guy who wakes up every morning and goes for a run, and has been doing so for ten years, rarely experiences resistance in the morning when it is time to go for that run. He has forged a powerful positive habit and it is now (almost) effortlessly more powerful than resistance. But those of us who don't exercise as much as we should experience all kinds of resistance every time we even think about exercising. Our to-do list and any number of distractions immediately steal our attention away from the idea of working out.

Over time what I realized was that John was trying to help me develop habits of the inner life. We all have habits of the outer life, good and bad. And we all have habits of the inner life, good and bad. Negative habits of mind, body, and spirit are easily formed. Positive habits of the mind, body, and soul require great intentionality and persistence. But once gained they are like ground that is won forever. We must still be vigilant, but the hardest yards have been won.

People often say, "Oh, I wish I could be young again." I don't. Too much ground has been won. Much of it has been hard won, and at great cost. I wouldn't want to give it up and have to fight for it all over again. I wouldn't want to have to write this book again. I hear about authors losing whole manuscripts and I cringe at the thought. If I lost the only copy of a complete manuscript, I am not sure I could write it again. One of the things I love about writing a book is that once it is finished, it can never be taken away from me. It is there for anyone to read. It is ground that has been gained and won, and cannot be lost.

Habits that help us become the-very-best-version-of-ourselves are beautiful things. I want my children to develop good, strong habits. That doesn't make me unique or special. All parents have this desire for their children. Made in the image and likeness of God, we get this instinct from him. Just as we want our children to develop good, strong habits, God wants us to do the same as his children. He passes his parental instincts along to you and me.

Here in this small volume, I am offering you some life-changing inner habits. There is no speculation here. These are not new fads or the latest trend. These are tried-and-true methods that have been helping people to master resistance for thousands of years. I hope as you have read this book you have been able to take an inventory of your life, the good, the bad, and the ugly. Never get discouraged. Remember, every moment is a chance to turn it all around. If you don't like what you find when you take an inventory of your life, start developing a great new habit today.

Strong habits will help you break through resistance. Good habits effortlessly defeat it.

⊛ KEY POINT
Habits—good and bad—have an enormous impact on our lives.

⚡ ACTION STEP
Write down your three best habits. Now write down three habits that you need to change.

---

(22)

How Many
Sundays Left?

My brother Simon is thirteen years older than I am. When I was a child he used to sell life insurance, and he later went on to become a financial adviser. Today he trains financial planners. I dedicated *The Dream Manager* to him, because in many ways he was the first person to play this role in my life in a more formal way. He has a lot of stories, analogies, and paradigms that he uses to illustrate his philosophy about life and business. One of my favorites is about Sundays.

How many Sundays do you have left?

I am 42 years old. The actuaries at the life insurance companies tell us that on average an Australian male lives for 80 years, four years longer than an American male, whose life expectancy is 76. On average an American female lives to 81. These life-expectancy statistics are always changing. For example, in the year 1900 the average life expectancy was just 31 years. This impacted all sorts of things. When people only lived to 31 they tended to get married younger and have children earlier. And perhaps one of the reasons there was less divorce was because marriages were shorter.

Anyway, Simon loves to talk about how many Sundays are left. At 42 years of age with a life expectancy of 78, I have 1,820 Sundays left. It sounds like a lot, but they go quickly.

As Simon loves to say, "Don't waste a single Sunday. If you don't waste Sundays, you will be less likely to waste Mondays Tuesdays, Wednesdays . . ."

⊛ **KEY POINT**
Life is short. Never waste a day.

⚡ **ACTION STEP**
Based on actuarial estimates, how many Sundays do you have left? Count them.

---

(23)

Attempted Murder

Our culture is trying to murder truth. It doesn't believe in objective truth. We have fallen into this ridiculous relativism that says, "What's true for you is true for you, and what's true for me is true for me." In other words, there is no objective truth. Nothing is true for everyone. Your opinion is your opinion and my opinion is my opinion. Truth is relative. So I may say 1 + 1 = 2, but you may say that 1 + 1 = 3.

This, of course, is absurd. Some things are true and the same for everyone. Gravity is one example. It is true for everybody. If you jump from a building you will fall to the ground. Saying gravity does not exist or that you do not acknowledge gravity does not change reality. People need water and air to live. This is an objective truth. Water freezes once it is chilled to a certain temperature. This is true for everyone, everywhere.

This nonsense that simply thinking something makes it true reminds me of a bumper sticker I saw once that read, **GOD IS DEAD. NIETZSCHE.** Then below that it read, **NIETZSCHE IS DEAD. GOD.**

In order to consistently overcome resistance we need to give truth a place of honor in our lives.

In order to consistently experience the happiness and joy God wants to fill us with we need to build a throne for truth in our lives. There is a direct relationship between truth and happiness. Truth leads to happiness. Lies bring misery.

Celebrate truth in your life. What place does it have in your life? Are you willing to speak truth even at great personal cost? Are you able to acknowledge truth, even if you cannot live up to it? Even if we cannot do something that is good, even if we willfully and sinfully choose to do something that is wrong, we should still try to acknowledge what is good and true, rather than trying to justify our behavior. It is easy to fall into the trap of thinking that because we can't live up to a truth we should deny it or, worse, attack it.

Where are you allowing lies to take root in your life?

When we resist truth we resist God and we resist happiness. We cannot be happy separated from the truth; we cannot be happy in a world of lies.

Of course, in the end, truth will prevail. But in the meantime, our refusal to acknowledge and celebrate it will cause an awful lot of people to suffer in unimaginable ways.

Our culture is trying to murder truth and it is important to note that you cannot murder truth without first murdering the Catholic Church. So in a culture that hates truth, the Catholic Church is public enemy number one.

Earlier this year I was reflecting upon these themes around the same time that the design team asked me to write a message for our Easter card. This is what I came up with:

One Friday afternoon they nailed truth to a tree.
But on Sunday morning, truth rose from the dead.
You cannot kill truth.
You can put it in a tomb, but you cannot keep it there.
May the Way, the Truth, and the Life of Jesus Christ
rise up in you this Easter.

Our culture is trying to murder truth. It will fail. But sadly, millions of people are suffering every day from the confusion that this assault on truth is creating.

All we can do is give truth a primary place of honor in our lives. Speak the truth. Live the truth. Celebrate truth. When we lie we not only resist happiness, we repel it.

⭐ KEY POINT
Our culture is trying to murder truth.

⚡ ACTION STEP
Give truth a place of honor in your heart, mind, and soul by telling the truth. Next time you catch yourself about to tell a lie, pause. Ask yourself why you are lying.

---

(24)

Hungry

We are all hungry for something. Figuring out what we are really hungry for is one of the great spiritual quests of life. There are so many different types of hunger. There is, of course, the natural hunger for food, but most of us are rarely hungry for food. In fact, our tendency to overeat often limits our ability to work out what we are really hungry for. Some people are hungry for comfort; others are hungry to belong; still others for success, sex, safety, adventure, security, travel. To be human is to be hungry.

Do you know what you are hungry for?

It takes an incredible spiritual awareness to work out over time what we are really hungry for. We may think that our hunger is for one thing, but once we have had our fill of that thing, we discover that the hunger is still there and deeper than ever.

Hunger is one of the central themes in *A Moveable Feast*, Ernest Hemingway's memoir of his time in Paris as a young man. He speaks about the role hunger plays in the creative process. In modern times those who become incredibly successful also often become soft and comfortable, and are accused of having lost their hunger—the hunger to win, the hunger for excellence, the hunger to be the best, or the hunger to be great.

Hemingway writes about a day he spent walking around Paris with his wife, Hadley. As they walked past the restaurant Michaud's, they saw the patrons enjoying their meals. Ernest and Hadley decided to splurge and have a feast. He ate like a king, but on the way home realized that the hunger was still there. He thought it was a hunger for food, but it was something subtler and more elusive. At home he made love to his wife, and lying there afterward in the dark, again he realized that he was still hungry.

There were many days during his Paris years when he didn't eat at all. Hemingway closes the book, which was written more than thirty years after the events it describes, by saying, "Those were the days when we were very poor and very happy." Hunger is so much more complex than simply desiring food. As we become more comfortable in this world, we tend to have an abundance of food and of so many things that it can be hard for us to hear our hunger. Our hunger speaks to us in a thousand languages.

What is the purpose of hunger? Every yearning we experience as human beings is a yearning for something more complete.

The ultimate spiritual awareness leads us to understand that every yearning is in some mysterious way a yearning for God. While we are searching for him far and wide in this world, he is waiting for us in the very depths of our souls. But in the early stages of spiritual development it is enough to recognize that God speaks to us in our hunger. He uses our hunger to teach us and guide us.

Are you able to look back on other times in your life and see that God was speaking to you through your hunger? What is he saying to you now through your hunger?

Is hunger good or bad? It can be either. Like so many things, it all depends on how we respond to it. Resistance loves hunger. It plays on our hunger, uses it to distract us, and worse, uses it to lead us to procrastination and inaction, to laziness and nothingness. But this is not the intended purpose of our hunger. God uses our hunger to lead us to him. Our neediness hunger is always a reminder that our ever-present need is for God.

I love food. I eat when I am happy and I eat when I am sad. I eat when I am anxious and when I am content. I eat to celebrate. I eat to reward myself and I eat to console myself. There are very few occasions that don't equate to eating for me. When I am packing for a trip, I think about the food I will eat.

Name a city anywhere in the world and I can probably tell you where you should eat—everything from fine restaurants to the best street food and, of course, where to find the best chocolate. In Paris, you should have breakfast at La Bauhinia, lunch at Maison de Gyros, and dinner at Le Lobby, and pick up a box of chocolates from La Maison du Chocolat. In Pittsburgh, dinner at the Grand Concourse and chocolates at Betsy Ann. In Sydney, pick up some chocolate from Haigh's in the Strand Arcade, have lunch at the Bluewater Café on Manly Beach or incredible Chinese cuisine at the East at Circular Quay, then for dinner visit Cafe Sydney, ARIA, or Doyles at Watsons Bay. I could write a book just about food and another about chocolate, but I hope you would agree that this would be a massive misappropriation of time and talent.

The point is I love food. Even a visit to the supermarket is an interesting study. To begin, let me confess that I very, very rarely go to the supermarket. But about once a year, my wife will ask me to go and grab something that was forgotten or that we ran out of. I always return with delicacies from every department in the store. It's probably one of the reasons I am rarely sent to the grocery store.

And of course, with all these little kids running around at the Kelly house, I have had my fair share of children's shows over the past six years. Too often I find myself agreeing with Winnie the Pooh: "What could be more important than a little something to eat?"

Am I hungry for food? Absolutely not. So, what am I hungry for? There are a thousand theories. Some would say I am hungry to release stress and tension, and others would say I am hungry for a more balanced life. Some would just say I have a problem with self-control, and while I know that is part of it, I also know it is much more complex than that. Something is triggering this behavior.

What I know for certain is that my relationship with food is unhealthy. The primary purpose of food is to fuel the body; its secondary purpose is pleasure. But I often reverse the order. My relationship with food is a lot more complex than I can summarize in a few paragraphs, but the bottom line is I want food to do things for me that it is not designed to do.

I struggle with this unhealthy relationship every day, and too often I allow resistance to use food to defeat me. People judge me. They send me letters or e-mails telling me that I need to lose weight. They come up to me at events and say things like, "You have really gained some weight" or "How's your health? You seem heavier than last time I heard you speak." Or they tell me about some great new diet or weight-loss program. They accuse me of being inauthentic and not living the message I share. It is humbling and humiliating.

We are all struggling with something. This is my thing. Saint Paul spoke about the thorn in his side: "To keep me from becoming too conceited, I was given a thorn in my flesh" (2 Corinthians 12:7). For two thousand years scholars have been debating about what they think Paul's struggle was. Some think it was a sexual obsession or weakness. Others think it was a pride or ego battle. We will never know. But we do know everyone struggles with something.

Paul also spoke about his struggle to do what he knew was good and right: "For I do not do the good I want, but the evil I do not want is what I do" (Romans 7:19). It sounds like Paul had his fair share of tussles with resistance too.

Every day people write to me about their struggles. In many cases the people around them don't know what they are struggling with. Just today I heard from a woman who became pregnant when she was sixteen and gave her daughter up for adoption. She is fifty now, and every day for more than thirty years she has wondered what happened to her daughter. I also had an e-mail from a man who is struggling with an addiction to pornography and a woman who had an abortion thirty years ago, needs healing, and doesn't know where to turn; a father who is dying from cancer, hasn't spoken to his son in thirty years, and doesn't know how to reach out even now at the end; and a woman who has stolen about two hundred thousand dollars from her employer and gambled it all away. These are just today's stories and struggles. Everyone is indeed fighting a hard battle, carrying a heavy load.

We are all struggling with something. Some of our struggles are easier to hide than others. My struggle with food is there for all to see. Others can hide their struggles. But sometimes being able to hide our struggles makes them harder, not easier.

What's your thing? Whatever it is, name it, right now. Just naming resistance causes it to lose much of its power over us. And simply naming what we are struggling with helps us to start down a healthier road.

⭐ **KEY POINT**
We are all hungry for something.

⚡ **ACTION STEP**
Write down everything you are hungry for at this time in your life.

Breaking the Cycle

There was only one time in those early days, when I was really starting to take the inner life seriously, that I came to John and said, "Okay. What's next?" I think I was immediately sorry that I did. But what he shared with me that day is one of the indispensable lessons of the spiritual life.

We all encounter things that bring us to our knees. Sooner or later a situation arises in which we feel completely helpless. In Mark's Gospel, there is a beautiful story about a man who brought his possessed boy to Jesus for healing. The father explained that he had brought his son to Jesus' disciples but they were unable to heal him, even though they had been able to heal many others with similar afflictions. When Jesus arrived at this scene, he rebuked the unclean spirit, ordering it to come out of the boy, and the child was cured. The disciples were confused about why they had not been able to cast out the demon. So, when the crowd had dispersed and they were alone with Jesus, "his disciples asked him in private, 'Why was it that we could not cast it out?' And he told them, 'This kind of spirit can only be cast out through prayer and fasting'" (Mark 9:28–29).

We all have demons that we need Jesus to cast out. Breaking the cycle of self-sabotage and self-destructive behavior is never easy. These behaviors make us intimately aware of our own broken humanity. Then we have two choices: We can arrogantly and stubbornly hold on to our self-destructive ways or we can turn to God and ask for help.

One of the most successful spiritual movements of the twentieth century is Alcoholics Anonymous. It has helped millions of men and women to get sober and stay sober, but more than that, it has given them back their lives.

The first three steps of the AA twelve-step process are:
1. We admitted we were powerless over alcohol—that our lives had become unmanageable.
2. Came to believe that a power greater than ourselves could restore us to sanity.
3. Made a decision to turn our will and our lives over to the care of God as we understood him.

They admitted they were powerless. What are you powerless over? They conceded that their lives had become unmanageable. Is some area of your life unmanageable? They acknowledged that God could restore them to sanity. Do you need God to restore sanity to some area of your life? They turned their lives and their will over to God. Thy will be done.

We all have cycles of thought or behavior that need to be broken. We have all tried to break these cycles over and over again, and failed over and over again.

Addiction in all its forms, large and small, serious and less serious (no addiction is trivial), is one of the central themes of our lives. Identifying our own addictions of thought and action is part of each person's spiritual journey. Food, control, talking too much, work, sex, pornography, alcohol, drugs, always being right, noise, negative thinking, negative humor, skepticism, cynicism, minimalism . . . the list is varied and endless. It doesn't matter what it is for you, and it doesn't matter what it is for me. What matters is how we respond.

I had grown up Catholic. I had been to Catholic schools my whole life. We had eaten fish on Fridays and given up chocolate for Lent. But nobody had ever spoken to me about fasting. It had never been explained to me that fasting goes way beyond food; that we can fast from anything. It is as if one of the most powerful tools in the spiritual life had been kept from me.

John encouraged me to start giving up little things each day. If you want a Coke, have water. If you want the steak, have the salmon. If you want to take a shortcut, go the long way. If you want to cut a conversation short, hear the person out. If you want to stop working, push yourself to go on for another thirty minutes.

Give up the little things, not to punish yourself, but as a short prayer and to strengthen your will. Always accompanied with a short prayer: "Lord, I will have the water even though I am craving the Coke. I offer this tiny sacrifice as a prayer for my friend who is struggling with cancer. Amen." Tiny sacrifices are offered to God as a prayer for specific intentions.

By denying ourselves in these small ways, we also strengthen our will, which increases our ability to love God and others. To love is to freely give ourselves to another. In order to freely give ourselves, we must first possess ourselves. So we can only love another to the extent that we are free.

Any type of inner slavery limits our ability to love ourselves, to love God, and to love others.

God wants to strengthen your will each day. He wants you to have an incredibly strong will. Then he wants you to surrender entirely to his will.

Some cycles in our lives can only be broken by prayer and fasting. We need to beg God in prayer to help us overcome the self-sabotaging cycles in our lives. And there are a hundred opportunities to deny ourselves in small ways.

Breaking down the destructive cycles in our lives is never easy. It is not something we can do on our own. We need the encouragement and prayers of the people around us, and we need the grace of God. When we face these cycles of self-sabotage and destruction we very quickly become convinced that there is such a thing as the grace of God, and that we need it.

⭐ **KEY POINT**
We are all struggling with something. Identify your something. Name it. Own it.

⚡ **ACTION STEP**
Pray and fast, asking God to liberate you from that area of slavery in your life.

You Cannot Succeed at Anything Without . . .

One of the many things I love about Catholicism is that it truly does bridge heaven and earth—not just in a theological way, but in a real and practical way. The simple habit of self-denial is a spiritual habit, but it has tremendous implications for our worldly affairs. Self-denial leads to the immensely practical skill of delaying gratification.

The ability to delay gratification is intimately linked with success. You cannot succeed at anything unless you are willing and able to delay gratification.

In order to have a healthy financial life that balances earning with spending, and saving with giving, one must be able to delay gratification. In order to raise children to become the-best-version-of-themselves, one must be willing to delay gratification. Great marriages are built on individual and mutual delayed gratification. Great careers are built little by little over time, and require doing the hard yards early and delaying gratification.

Self-denial is essential to spiritual growth. In order to become our best self we must deny our lesser self. We deny our false self to find our true self.

A couple of months ago I was with a group of friends who were talking about a television show. They have seen every episode, many of them several times. They know the characters and the scenes intimately. I had no idea what they were talking about. As the conversation went on, someone had the awareness to realize I was lost, and asked, "Do you like the show?" I had to explain to them that I had never seen it. They were all in disbelief.

As I drove home I thought about it some more. The show was immensely popular during the 1990s. I spent the '90s on the road. And I am not sorry I did. If I had to trade a few episodes of a television show that was literally about nothing for my experiences on the road, then so be it. In fact, if I had to trade every single episode of that show for my time on the road I would. Those years traveling have made so many things possible for me and for Dynamic Catholic. Were those years easy? No. Did they involve a great many sacrifices? Absolutely. I sacrificed things like watching television shows and hanging out in clubs and bars with my friends, but I'm okay with that.

The ability to delay gratification is an elevated spiritual discipline, but it is also an immensely practical skill.

During the 1960s and '70s a well-known series of studies on delayed gratification, now known as the Stanford marshmallow experiment, was conducted by psychologist Walter Mischel, who was at the time a professor at Stanford University. In these studies, a child was offered a choice between receiving a treat such as a marshmallow or a cookie immediately, or receiving two treats if he waited approximately fifteen minutes. The tester would leave the first treat on the desk and leave the room for fifteen minutes. The child was instructed that if he wished to have two treats instead of the one, simply to leave the first treat on the desk.

It was an astoundingly simple test. And yet, all these years later, in follow-up studies, the researchers have found that children who were able to wait longer for the preferred rewards tended to have better life outcomes, as measured by SAT scores, educational attainment, general health and well-being, and other life measures.

On the day you decide to intentionally start denying yourself, your life will improve in a thousand ways. It is a lesson I am now trying to figure out how best to teach my children. It is not about saying no to them; it is about teaching them to say no to themselves. These realizations about denying ourselves, self-control, delayed gratification, and fasting are not new. They are wrapped up in two thousand years of Catholic genius. Saint Augustine wrote, "Conquer yourself and the world lies at your feet."

Several years ago, I was in Washington, D.C., doing a presentation for a group of about two hundred entrepreneurs and business owners, and I heard a great story from one of the attendees, a gentleman named Mike.

Mike and his two best friends were turning forty, and because of the pressure of work and family he had fallen out of shape. So they decided to get into shape together. This was going to be the year.

So these three guys signed up for a get-fit program run by a retired army sergeant. The program was ninety minutes three days a week—Monday, Wednesday, and Friday—starting at six thirty a.m.

By lunchtime the first day, Mike said, he could hardly move. When he woke up the next morning and tried to get out of bed his body refused. The contortions that followed in order for him to get his two feet on the floor had his wife howling with laughter.

On the first day of the second week, Mike was not feeling that well. The first week had taken it out of him, he had spent the weekend running around to events with the kids, and he and his wife went to big party Saturday night, where he proceeded to drink too much.

About fifteen minutes into the class that Monday morning he approached the sergeant and requested permission to sit out for five minutes and catch his breath. "No," was the sergeant's answer.

"But I have a cramp and I think I need to stretch it out," Mike complained.

"No, that's not your problem," the sergeant replied.

"What is my problem?" Mike asked, regretting having asked as soon as the words crossed his lips.

"Your problem is, you are very fat, you're very lazy, and you are mentally weak. Now, shake it off and get back in there before I make you give me a hundred push-ups."

You may not be physically fat, but we all probably have a bit of spiritual obesity that needs to be dealt with. We can all be lazy from time to time, both physically and spiritually. And we can all fall into the trap of a soft, weak mind if we are not careful.

Resistance hates discipline. It hates self-control. Resistance abhors delayed gratification and any

type of self-denial that makes your heart, mind, and soul strong.

God wants us to have a strong mind, a strong heart, and a spirit that soars with so much strength that nothing in this world can weigh it down. These things can only be accomplished with prayer and fasting.

⭐ **KEY POINT**

You cannot succeed at anything unless you are willing to delay gratification. This ability and success are intimately linked.

⚡ **ACTION STEP**

Say no to yourself at least once every day.

㉗
The Secret to Excellence

I have seven brothers: Mark, Simon, Andrew, Brett, Nathan, Bernard, and Hamish. Growing up in Australia, all we did was play sports. What sports? Any sport. Football, cricket, tennis, soccer, swimming, running, basketball, volleyball, golf, table tennis, biking—you name it, we probably gave it a try. Were we competitive? Yes we were. Ultracompetitive. I still remember getting thrown in the pool during a cricket match in the backyard when my brothers didn't like the call. We played sports all the time.

My father loved sports and one of his favorite things to do was watch his sons play. I believe it gave him a tremendous sense of pride and filled him with great joy to watch his boys out there competing.

I began playing competitive sports when I was five years old. Every time I went to training and every time I went to a game, my dad said the very same thing to me: "Matthew, listen to your coach!" Every time. He never forgot. If he was traveling, he would call me on the phone sometimes before a game to wish me well, and to remind me to listen to my coach.

When I was about sixteen years old, he was dropping me off for a soccer game while he went and parked the car. As I walked away from the car, he put down the window and said, "Matthew, don't forget—" I interrupted him and said, "I got it, Dad—listen to my coach, listen to my coach, listen to my coach!"

A few weeks later, Dad and I were talking and I asked him, "Dad, why do you always say, 'Listen to your coach'?"

He didn't miss a beat. He looked me straight in the eye and said, "Because nobody achieves excellence at anything without coaching."

"What do you mean?" I asked.

"You can get good at something just by working hard at it. If you've got some talent and you work hard at it, you can get really, really good at it. But excellence, peak performance, being the best you can be at something—that doesn't happen without coaching."

My father was a student of excellence. He loved excellence, wherever it could be found. He would point it out to us, in business, in sports, in the arts, in politics, spiritually and academically. He was a student of excellence and he taught us to be students of excellence too.

So, here's my question: Whom do you get your spiritual coaching from? If we are going to grow spiritually, if we are going to become excellent in the spiritual life, we need coaching.

The sad truth is, when it comes to our Catholicism, we don't think about it in those terms. When was the last time someone said to you, "I really want to be an excellent Catholic"? Maybe never. Excellence isn't even on our radar. As a result, we now live in a time when, as Catholics living in the United States, we have become deeply committed to our mediocrity. We stopped striving for inner, spiritual excellence, and because the external is an overflow of the internal, we started doing things in a mediocre way. Everything we do as Catholics should be excellent, but we do a lot of things mediocre. We all want to belong to excellent parishes, but we don't necessarily want to strive for spiritual excellence.

Where is the excellence? What do we do in a truly world-class and excellent way as Catholics? There are some things. We are the best in the world at caring for the poor, but we could do more. We are the best in the world at education, but our education has become financially inaccessible to the average Catholic family. But truth be told, it is a relatively short list of things that we do in an excellent way—and everything we do as Catholics should be excellent.

If you want to be part of an excellent parish, stop waiting for someone else to make it one. Get involved and make it an excellent parish. Resistance encourages us to take it easy and settle for mediocrity. But God created us for happiness, and he fills us with great joy as we strive for excellence, especially in the spiritual life.

It's strange, as I look back, that before I met John, nobody ever talked to me about excellence in the spiritual life. I never heard a homily about it. Nobody ever says, "You can become a saint!" I didn't know that everyone could be holy. I didn't know that God was calling me to live a holy life. I didn't know that holiness was even a possibility for people like you and me. I guess I thought Christianity was just about being a nice person and telling the truth. But it turns out we are all called to holiness. We are all called to become the-best-version-of-ourselves. We can make all sorts of excuses about why we cannot, but that doesn't change the fact that the central goal of the Christian life is to love God and neighbor by living a holy life. When we lose sight of that, we become spiritually lost. Better to be physically blind than spiritually lost.

God wants you to live an excellent life. In that quest for excellence you will find a rare happiness.

⭐ **KEY POINT**
Nobody achieves excellence at anything without coaching.

⚡ **ACTION STEP**
Seek out a spiritual coach.

---

(28)

The Light Is On

"When's the last time you went to confession?" John asked.

"What, no small talk today? We're just launching into the big stuff. Don't you want to know how my prayer life is, or if I have been studying hard?" I pushed back.

The truth is I was taken by surprise and I was deflecting. But he just waited patiently, letting the question linger in the air. As he remained silent, I began to think about it. I couldn't remember. At least, I wasn't sure. "I think it was on the last youth group retreat."

Talk about resistance. If there is one battle that resistance has dominated in the hearts and minds of Catholics for the past fifty years, it surrounds confession. We just stopped going. On one level it makes complete sense. When you stop striving for excellence, you stop yearning for coaching. Mediocrity seeks comfort and going to confession isn't comfortable. It's uncomfortable to look at ourselves, assess our selfishness and sinfulness, and tell another human being about it. But wow, is it good for us.

We all have a great need for healing. We all need to be liberated from our self-centeredness.

We need to grow in awareness of how what we do and say affects the people around us and people on the other side of the world. But we resist it. We resist God. We resist his forgiveness. We resist happiness.

Saint Augustine prayed, "Lord, make me chaste, but not just yet." He loved loving women. He wasn't ready to give that up. He was resisting a-better-version-of-himself. As it turned out, he was resistant to becoming one of the greatest saints in the history of Christianity.

For more than twenty years I have been going to confession regularly. There is always a temptation to put it off. Resistance puts a barrier between me and going to confession, and as always I have to break through that barrier, slay resistance, and go. The interesting thing is, whenever I go I am always glad I went. Just like when it is time to work out we often don't feel like it, but we force ourselves to do it and we are always glad we did. You don't meet people who have been retired for a year who say, "I hate myself because I saved far too much money for retirement." When we save money we are always glad we did. We almost never regret delaying gratification. All of life's regrets come from not having the discipline to overcome resistance and delay gratification in order to build a bigger future. In the same way, when we slay resistance we are always glad we did.

I cannot say it any better than I did in *Rediscover Catholicism*.

Consider this analogy. How often do you wash your car, or have it washed? Perhaps once every two or three weeks, maybe once a month, but it is probably not ten years since you had your car washed! And when your car is all shiny and clean on the outside and clean and tidy on the inside, you feel pretty good about that. Driving a clean car feels different than driving a dirty car.

When you are driving home from the car wash with your clean car, what do you pray? You pray it doesn't rain, right? Or you at least think it, hope it! As if God doesn't have better things to worry about. There are fifty thousand people dying every day in Africa from extreme poverty and preventable disease, but you just got your ten-dollar car wash and you want that at the top of his list. In any event, it doesn't rain, but the next day you are driving down the road and there is a big puddle of mud right in the middle.

What do you do? You go around it, of course; you just got your car washed.

The day after that you think to yourself, *It might get cold later; I better take a jacket.* You take a jacket with you but you don't need it. So you say to yourself, *I'll put this in the backseat; I'll get it later.* Do you get it later? No.

The next day you think to yourself, *I have to go to the doctor today; I better take a book or a magazine with me, because they never seem to have any good magazines.* Besides, what type of people go to a doctor's office? That's right, sick people. Then they all gather together in a little room with six magazines and they touch those magazines with their sick fingers. When you get to the doctor's you pick up that magazine and look at the cover and it reads, "Issue 137, February 1983," and you think to yourself, *How many sick people have been here since February 1983?* You bring your own magazine and once you get done with your doctor's visit you put that magazine on the backseat of your car. You say to yourself, *I'll get it later.* But you don't.

The next day you are going somewhere and it's getting late, you are hungry, and you don't know when you are going to have a chance to eat. So you go to the drive-through and get whatever it is you get when you go to the drive-through. Now you are driving while eating, and you're talking on your cell phone, so you are steering with your knees. When you get done eating you say to yourself, *I won't put this trash on the backseat; I just got my car washed.* So you get all the trash from the meal and you stuff it back into the bag the food came in and say to yourself, *I'll just put this trash neatly on the floor in the backseat. I'll get it out as soon as I get home.* Do you? Probably not.

The following day you throw another little piece of junk into the backseat and the day after that you toss another piece back there. Before you know it, it's Sunday again, and you're coming home from Church, and what do you have now? That's right, you've got the bulletin, which you probably read while Father was giving his homily. So, you think to yourself, *I've already read this,* as you throw it over your shoulder into the backseat. The next day it's a gum wrapper or some other small bits of trash and the day after that it's one or two little bits of junk that you are moving from home to work or vice versa.

The next thing you know, two or three weeks have passed since you got your car washed. The car is quite messy on the inside and dirty on the outside, and you become less careful with it. You just throw another little piece of trash in the backseat because there is already so much that you won't notice the extra piece. And then, before long, you are throwing big bits of trash back there. Do you know why? Because you have lost your sensitivity, and once you lose that sensitivity a big piece of trash doesn't look that bad among all those little bits!

We lose our sensitivity to sin in exactly the same way. After a while, a big self-destructive behavior doesn't look that bad among all those little self-destructive behaviors.

When you get your car washed you are sensitive to the things that make it dirty. In the same way, after you have been to Confession you are sensitive to the things that stop you from being the-best-version-of-yourself. When you come out of Confession you are sensitive to the thoughts, words, actions, people, and places that will not help you to walk with God. I don't know how long that sensitivity lasts for you, but after a while it wears off and you become indifferent to the things that will not help you to live a life of holiness and be true to yourself.

Haven't you ever noticed the way people living good lives have a glow about them? They don't seem to be carrying the weight of the world on their shoulders. When you go to Confession your soul is cleansed and an inner beauty shines from within you. But after a few weeks, the little sins begin to pile up, and before you know it, a big sin doesn't look so bad on top of a pile of small sins. And once you add the big one to the pile, you figure you've made a mess already so you might as well really make a mess. Little by little, you begin to lose your sense of sin. Before you know it, you are very unhappy, and you don't really know why. You don't feel at peace with yourself and you find yourself becoming impatient and irritable with the people around you. You begin to experience a certain restlessness and anxiety, but you don't know what is causing it.

How long does this desensitization take? I suspect it is different for different people, and even different at various times in our lives. There have been times when I have struggled with habitual sins, even while trying to rid my life of them. During those times I have gone to Confession as often as every week. But now, at this time in my life, I lose that sensitivity after a month, so I have made a habit of going to Confession once a month. If I don't, I find I become inattentive and desensitized to the things that separate me from God, my neighbor, and my true self.

In addition to the incredible spiritual benefits of Reconciliation, once again we find an ancient spiritual experience that produces benefits that are incredibly practical right now. For example, and this is one of many, if you go to confession regularly you will have the best relationships you have ever had in your lifetime. By looking at ourselves and allowing God to help us grow, we develop incredible emotional intelligence and awareness that makes us much better friends, children, lovers, and parents. There is nothing more practical than great relationships.

The root of all my problems is selfishness.

This selfishness is, of course, a sure path to unhappiness, and it's the path resistance often recommends to me. Confessing helps me to cast off my selfishness and rearrange my priorities, bringing order and clarity to my life.

It doesn't matter how long it is since you have been—make a point in the next couple of weeks to go to confession. But let me prepare you. You will be surprised how difficult it is to go, from a logistical point of view. Every parish is different, but the one I am visiting this week has confessions on Saturday morning from eight thirty to nine, or by appointment. A few weeks ago I met a priest with a fabulous personality, full of joy, and he had these great one-liners for everything. Someone started talking about confession hours and he called these "the devil's hours." I asked him what he meant, and he went on to explain that if the devil were in charge of scheduling times for confession, he would schedule them to ensure that the very fewest people would go. To this end, the devil would probably schedule them on Saturday morning from eight thirty to nine.

Over the past three years there has been a fabulous initiative is dioceses in Ireland, the United States, and Australia called The Light Is On. Referring to the light that indicates that the priest is in the confessional and ready to hear your confession, these campaigns are an invitation for people to come back to Reconciliation. In a number of churches, which were widely advertised in advance, priests were available for confessions around the clock for two days. Anytime, day or night, people could drop into these churches and go to Reconciliation. In one diocese some priests even set up in the middle of the most popular shopping mall in the city and heard confessions during the mall's open hours. The response has been absolutely enormous.

The model of Jesus' ministry was to go to the people. We need to go out to the people again. They need God, his Church, and his people to minister to them.

There are four simple words I want to end this section with. A wise priest said them to me many, many years ago when I first started traveling around the world speaking. It was on one of my first trips to Ireland; we were having dinner one night after an event and I could tell he was concerned for me. "Be gentle with yourself, Matthew!" he said. At the time I brushed it off as being a little soft, maybe even weak. I didn't get it. Since then I have discovered how very difficult life really is. I have discovered how fragile we are as human beings. I have discovered that yes indeed, everyone you'll ever meet really is fighting a hard battle.

Four words: *Be gentle with yourself.* It turns out they are some of the wisest words anyone has ever shared with me. In turn, I have shared them with many others. It doesn't mean be soft with yourself, and it doesn't mean be undisciplined. Being gentle with yourself consists of realizing your faults, failings, and weaknesses, and dealing with them appropriately. God doesn't want us to beat ourselves up. He wants us to press on and try again. In the words of Saint Francis de Sales, "Have patience with all things, but chiefly have patience with yourself. Do not lose courage in considering your own imperfections but instantly set about redeeming them—every day begin anew."

One of the most important reasons to be gentle with ourselves is because if we cannot forgive ourselves, we will struggle to forgive others. And if we cannot forgive ourselves or others, we will resist even God's forgiveness. When we are gentle with ourselves, when we are patient with ourselves, we develop awareness, and awareness breeds compassion. And every person who ever crosses your path needs a little compassion.

Be gentle with yourself, be gentle with others, and never stop striving to be all that God created you to be: the-very-best-version-of-yourself.

⭐ **KEY POINT**

We all have a great need for forgiveness and healing.

⚡ **ACTION STEP**

No matter how long it has been, go to Reconciliation this week.

---

(29)

Are You a Pilgrim or a Tourist?

My good friend Father Bob Sherry and I have been hosting pilgrimages for a long, long time. Our current schedule includes three trips each year: the Holy Land; Lourdes and Paris, in France; and Rome, Assisi, and Florence, in Italy. On the opening night as we welcome the pilgrims, we always ask them the same question:

Are you going to be a pilgrim or are you going to be a tourist?

Tourists want everything to go exactly as they have planned and imagined it. They rush around from one place to another making sure they cram everything in. They are constantly buying souvenirs and knickknacks, many of which they will look at when they get home and wonder, "What was I thinking?" Tourists get upset if there are delays. They demand prompt attention and service to their every need and desire. They focus on themselves, often shoving past others to get where they want to go. Tourists go sightseeing. Tourists count the cost.

Pilgrims are very different. They look for signs. If a flight gets delayed or canceled, they ask, "What is God trying to say to me?" Pilgrims are not concerned with seeing and doing everything, just the things they feel called to see and do. They are not obsessed with shopping. They are aware of the needs of others. Pilgrims go looking for meaning. Pilgrims count their blessings.

The reality is we are all pilgrims. This planet we call earth is not our home; we are just passing through. We build homes and establish ourselves here on earth in ways that ignore that we are really just here for a short time. It is a dangerous pastime to live as if you were never going to die, but consciously or subconsciously we all fall into this trap to various degrees.

We are only here on earth for the blink of an eye. This is not our home. That's why the happiness that God wants and created us for is very different from the fleeting happiness and momentary pleasures of this world.

God created us for lasting happiness in a changing world and eternal happiness with him in heaven. The happiness he wants for us in this life is a rare kind of happiness that is not dependent on situations or circumstances. It is easy to be happy when everything is going well. But Christian joy allows us to be happy like Paul was when he was in prison.

Do you ever think about heaven? It seems to me we don't talk about it anywhere near as much as we should. When Rudyard Kipling was very seriously ill a nurse asked him, "Is there anything you want?" He replied, "I want God!" We all do. We may not be aware of it, but we want God. Behind every desire for a new car or a new house, a promotion or accomplishment, clothes and jewelry, plastic surgery, adventure and travel, food and sex, acceptance and comfort, is our desire for God. We are always hungry for something more complete, and God is that completeness that we yearn for from the depths of our soul.

We are just passing through, and it is helpful to remind ourselves of that from time to time. In the context of eternity, we are only here for the blink of an eye. Realizing this changes our priorities. At the same time, we are here for a reason. You are here for a reason. God has a mission for you.

Life is a pilgrimage, a sacred journey. Typically, a pilgrimage is a journey to a shrine or other location important to a person's faith or beliefs. You can make a pilgrimage to the Holy Land, Rome, Fatima, Lourdes, the Camino, or any of the famous Catholic sites around the world. But you could also make a pilgrimage to your nearest Cathedral. In fact, every Sunday you make a pilgrimage to your local parish for Mass.

Very often people make pilgrimages with special intentions in mind. Some ask God for a favor, perhaps to heal a loved one who is sick. Others make a pilgrimage in thanksgiving for a blessing they have already received from God. There are always couples on your trips who are celebrating a wedding anniversary. They are making the trip to thank God for their marriage. On every trip, Father Bob chooses one of the holy places and invites every couple on the trip to renew their marriage vows. Powerful! I cannot even describe how powerful and moving this is. I have seen it many times, but still it moves me. Sometimes people make a pilgrimage seeking clarity on some decision they have to make.

Life is a pilgrimage, but sometimes you need a pilgrimage to discover life. We are journeying in this life toward the sacred city, toward the heart of God—heaven. Nobody makes the journey alone. We all need companions. Some of my very best friends in this world I met on pilgrimages. These trips that Dynamic Catholic hosts are life changing, and when you experience something like that with other people, you form a very special bond.

The best friends in the world encourage us and challenge us to become the-best-version-of-ourselves, and by doing so, they help us to get to heaven.

Let us pray for the grace to be pilgrims and not just tourists. Let us pray for the grace to be the kind of friend who helps others in the great pilgrimage of life.

This is "A Pilgrim's Prayer," by Thomas Merton:

> My Lord God,
> I have no idea where I am going.
> I do not see the road ahead of me.
> I cannot know for certain where it will end. . . .
> Nor do I really know myself,
> And the fact that I think I am following Your will
> Does not mean that I am actually doing so.
> But I believe that the desire to please You does in fact
> please You.

And I hope I have that desire in all that I am doing.
I hope that I will never do anything apart from that desire.
And I know that if I do this,
You will lead me by the right road, though I may know nothing about it.
Therefore will I trust You always though I may seem lost
And in the shadow of death.
I will not fear, for You are ever with me,
And You will never leave me to face my perils alone.

⊘ **KEY POINT**
We are just passing through this place we call earth. We are pilgrims.

⊘ **ACTION STEP**
Spend some time today thinking about heaven.

---

(30)

The First Intervention

There have been two great interventions in my life. The first began on that Sunday afternoon at the barbecue when John stepped into my life, and it lasted about two years. The second lasted just one weekend. Both had a tremendous impact on my life.

As we each look back, we can see people who have made great contributions to our lives in different ways. John was a friend of my soul. I am convinced that we all need someone like this in our lives to help us get our inner lives firmly established. And we are all called to be this person for others. I have tried to be this person for others, and I hope at some point you will too.

John took me step-by-step through the basics of Catholic spirituality, patiently answered my questions, prayed for me every day, and held me accountable. He knew the path. Someone had taught him and now he was teaching me, and I have spent most of my life leading others to the path. John was trying to give me what he already had. It wasn't theory. Someone had walked alongside him and helped him to develop a rich spiritual life and a profound relationship with God. Now he was offering that to me. I should have run toward him and received what he was offering with arms wide open, but I was resistant. Resistance is in us all and always rears its ugly head with renewed enthusiasm when our lives are really about to change for the better.

Woven in between all the thought and reflections, ideas and stories that make up this book are the habits that became the foundation of my spiritual life for the past twenty-five years. They are tried and true. They work. I resisted them at first, and still resist them some days all these years later. They are without a doubt a strong foundation upon which anyone could build a deep and vibrant relationship with God.

I thought it might be good to see those habits all together in one place. Looking back, I see it as a beautiful process that allowed me to discover God and myself in exceptional ways, even though the process itself is very ordinary.

The journey John led me on was at one level quite simple and ordinary; on another level it was profound and completely transformational. Let's revisit the steps together.

- Believe: Have faith that holiness is possible, and that everything you do every day leads you closer to or further from the-very-best-version-of-yourself and the holy life God wants for you.
- Ten minutes a day: Create a daily habit of prayer.
- Hour by hour: Offer every hour of your life to God as a prayer, especially your work.
- Feed your mind: Spend time reading the Bible and other great spiritual books.
- Serve powerfully: Get outside yourself by finding ways to make a difference in the lives of others.

- Mass: Attend daily Mass once or twice during the week to develop a deeper love and understanding of this great mystery.
- Fasting: Deny yourself in small ways many times a day so that God can fill you with incredible spiritual strength.
- Reconciliation: Confess your sins regularly and open yourself up to spiritual coaching.

It is a simple process, and yet life changing. Imagine if we were all taught as children to establish these habits in our lives. How vibrant would your parish be? How vibrant would the Catholic Church in the United States be?

Well, it's not too late. Begin to establish these habits in your life. As they become strong in your life, help others to know them and to live them.

How would your life be different if you integrated these habits? Give them a chance. I promise you God will gift you through these habits in ways you cannot even imagine yet. Don't try to force them all into your life at once. Work your way through them, one at a time. Establish one as a firm habit, and then move on to the next one.

These are the steps that worked for me. I am not saying that this is the only path, or that it is for everyone. It may not be for everyone; I don't know. But we all need a plan. What's yours?

Have you ever really had a plan for spiritual health and growth?

If you feel like something is missing in your life, if you feel like you need a fresh start, if you are craving something more, take this simple plan and give it a chance. I am confident God will use it to do wonderful things.

I have had some incredible spiritual experiences over the years, but it is the ordinary daily spiritual practices that matter most. These day-to-day encounters with God are a hundred times more important than the extraordinary graced-filled spiritual experiences that God gives us sometimes.

John invested in me in an incredibly selfless way. When I think of the millions of people who have read my books and heard me speak, when I look at all the good work Dynamic Catholic is doing, I know none of that would have happened if it weren't for John. He lived the life of a disciple. The power of one friendship can change the course of a life.

Your friendship with others is not to be taken lightly. You are changing the direction of your friends' lives, for better or for worse. Sooner or later, we all rise or fall to the level of our friendships.

Are you wondering what happened to John? Those first two years we had an intense friendship. After that he continued to practice as a doctor and we stayed in touch, though less frequently. He was very supportive of my writing and speaking, and continued to challenge me to strive for holiness and excellence. About a decade later he was ordained a Catholic priest and dedicated the rest of his life to helping hundreds of people discover the path he had shown me.

At the age of forty-eight, he suffered a massive heart attack and died. After my father-in-law, he was the healthiest person I knew. It was a huge shock and a great loss. I often experience pain when I think of him, because the last time I saw him we argued. There were things happening within the hierarchy of the church that were wrong, and I felt he was in a position to draw attention to them, so that change could occur. He kept saying, "I am just a simple priest—what can I do?" But I think we both knew that he was not just a simple priest; he was an extraordinary man, a priest who was greatly respected, and perhaps one of the few people who would have been listened to if he had spoken up about the things that were transpiring. Nonetheless, I regret having argued with him.

I miss my friend. I wish I could meet him for coffee and talk. I wish he could tell me what he knows from the other side. We talk about God as if we know him, and God has certainly revealed a great deal about himself to us. But think about everything we don't know about God. There must be so much more that we have not considered or cannot even comprehend. I wonder often what John would say if he could speak to me now.

People come into our lives for a reason. Some are messengers; other are teachers. Some are healers, and others are coaches and counselors. Some people come into our lives for only a season, but their fingerprints remain all over our lives until the end.

⭐ KEY POINT

What's your plan? Have you ever really had a plan for spiritual health and growth?

⚡ ACTION STEP

How are you going to grow spiritually over the next twelve months? Write down a plan.

---

(31)

A Weekend Away

When my beautiful Isabel was about three we were cuddling quietly on the couch one day. She is simply the best cuddler in the whole world. After a long time, she said to me, "Daddy, are you happy at me?" My eyes filled with tears and I cannot even describe the feeling in my heart. "Oh yes, my love. You have no idea how happy I am to have you in my life. Growing up I didn't have any sisters, and when the doctor told us we were having a little girl I was ecstatic. You are my beautiful girl, and I will always be happy you are in my life, darling." She pulled me even tighter, and I could feel it in my soul that she felt loved and accepted.

We all have a great need to belong, to be loved and accepted.

We all need people to do life with, friends to accompany us on the pilgrimage of life. One of the things we are all hungry for is connection. We are also hungry for community. But we live in a time of empty connections and shadow communities. We connect with people online, but that is not a real connection. We join communities online, but these are pretend communities that don't come close to fulfilling the legitimate needs we have. The only thing these online connections and communities prove is that as human beings we have an incredible need and hunger for meaningful interaction with each other.

My life has been rich with friendships. So many people have blessed me in so many ways with their time, their advice, their love, generosity, and friendship. What makes a great friend? Our best friends are those people who encourage and challenge us to become the-best-version-of-ourselves.

The second great intervention in my life came as unexpectedly as the first. At the time I was surprisingly content, really quite satisfied in many ways.

Let me share this, not to boast but as necessary context for the story I am about to tell you. I was in my midthirties and for fifteen years I had traveled well over 250 days a year trying to help people develop their own inner lives. I had written more than a dozen books, which had sold about ten million copies, been published in more than twenty languages, and had been featured on all the most prestigious best-seller lists. I had spoken in more than fifty countries to a collective audience of more than three million people. In my spare time, I had founded a very successful consulting company that had more than forty Fortune 500 clients and hundreds of small and midsize business clients. To be honest, I was feeling pretty good about myself.

What happened next was that a handful of my friends decided to go away on a golf trip and invited me to join them. It was just what I needed—a chance to get away, relax among friends, and get some fresh air and exercise.

When we checked in to the hotel on the first day, we agreed to meet at six p.m. for a drink. One of the guys had a huge suite, so we were going to meet there. Being a planner, I am usually about five or ten minutes early for things. But when I got there, everyone else was already there and I had the feeling that they had been talking about something before I arrived.

I poured myself a rum and Coke and sat down. In hindsight, the armchair that was empty was sort of the focal point of the whole room, and that was not a coincidence. As I sat down, they said, "So, there is something we want to talk to you about this weekend."

Still oblivious, I answered, "Sure, whatever you need. What is it?"

Jeremy, who had obviously been appointed spokesperson for the group, said, "We think you are wasting your life and you need to make some changes." You could have pushed me over with a feather. *Blindsided* doesn't even begin to describe what had just happened.

"Um, okay . . . so, what makes you feel that way?" Then they just all started chiming in.

"Man, you are always on the road. That's not healthy."

"You can't reach enough people live; you need to get off the road and harness technology."

"You need to slow down if you are ever going to have any chance at a normal life."

"You're not married because you don't stay still long enough to form a meaningful relationship."

"You won't do your best work until you sink some roots and get settled."

Wow. I couldn't breathe. I didn't know what to think or where to look. It was surreal. I sat there stunned for a while. I'm not sure how long, but it felt like a long time. When I gathered my thoughts a little I asked half-jokingly, "So what should I be thinking about so I don't waste the rest of my life?"

"We want you to think about how you can have one hundred times more impact over the next fifteen years than you did over the past fifteen years."

The rest of the weekend was a blur. I hit more golf balls into the water that weekend than I had in three years combined. Maybe that was part of their plan: Drop this on me to throw me off my game. But here's the thing. They were great friends. I knew that. I knew they had my best interests at heart. So I had to listen to them. And I did.

Dynamic Catholic exists because of that intervention. I was comfortable and satisfied, and looking back that should have set off alarm bells, but we all have blind spots.

Will this work God has entrusted to me and the team at Dynamic Catholic have one hundred times more impact in this fifteen-year period? It's impossible to say for sure, but I think it will. It will certainly come close. If it weren't for those friends, I would probably be out there doing the same old thing. That would be a tragedy. When I see all those young people who have moved from all over the country to be at Dynamic Catholic, I find that very humbling. I cannot imagine my life without Dynamic Catholic. It seems specially ordained to serve God's people in this way at this time.

Where did Dynamic Catholic come from? Well, my parents raised me and loved me, John challenged me to take the inner life seriously, and a bunch of guys confronted me about how my gifts could be used to achieve the most good for the most people. Thank God for interventions. Thank God for friends who care enough to intervene.

⭐ **KEY POINT**
Our best friends encourage and challenge us to become the-best-version-of-ourselves. They don't let us waste our lives and they push us to serve powerfully.

⚡ **ACTION STEP**
Who in your circle is God calling you to encourage or challenge to become a-better-version-of-themselves?

(32)

Let Your Light Shine

Luceat Lux Vestra. That was my high school motto. This Latin phrase, taken from Matthew's Gospel, means "Let your light shine." It has always stayed with me. The full verse reads, "Let your light shine before men, that they may see your good works and give glory to your Father in heaven" (Matthew 5:16).

Are you letting your light shine?

There are two things I find interesting in this one verse, beyond the obvious. The obvious is that God wants you to let your light shine. The less obvious is that Jesus assumes that you will do good works. He doesn't say, "If you do good works" or "On the chance that you get around to doing some good works in the midst of your very busy life." No, he assumes that you will do good works. You were made for good works. You were created to let your light shine.

Every person lets his or her light shine in different ways. Every person has a perfect mix of talents and abilities. The danger here is to fall into the trap of comparisons. Comparisons are worthless in a world of individuals. You are the perfect mix of talents and abilities to fulfill the mission that God has in mind for you. There is no point worrying about what talents and abilities other people have. If you don't have them, you don't need them for your mission. So get on out there and do good works. Let your light shine!

The other indirect insight this verse gives birth to in light of our discussion is that resistance wants to stop you from letting your light shine. Resistance always wants the opposite of what God wants. In Matthew 5:15, Jesus says, "Nobody lights a lamp and puts it under a bushel. They put it on a stand, so that it can give light to everyone in the house." This is common sense. But resistance is not reasonable or sensible. Resistance doesn't want you to light your lamp. It doesn't want you to put your lamp on a stand. It wants you to hide your light beneath a bushel. And it absolutely does not want you to let your light shine. But as we discussed in the beginning of this book, resistance wears a thousand masks. What stops you from letting your light shine? Fear, laziness, procrastination, selfishness, addiction, obsession, comparing yourself to others, allowing your critics to drain your energy and direct your life, an unwillingness to move beyond your comfort zone, self-doubt, gossip, negative relationships, worry, excuses, and so many others.

God wants to move you beyond all these bad habits of the mind, body, and soul, and fill you with his grace and courage so that you can go out into the world and let your light shine.

Each night before my children go to bed I spend a few minutes with each of them. They call it "special time," and different rituals have developed for each child during that time. Harry is two and a half at the moment, and one of the things he likes to do after we talk about his day and do our prayers is sing a song or two. Well, mostly I sing the song and he sings the last word of every phrase. There are a few songs in the repertoire, but every night when I ask him what songs he would like to sing he says, "Light of mine." This is his shorthand for the classic children's song "This Little Light of Mine." If I try to put him to bed without singing this song with him, he says, "Light of mine. Light of mine. Light of mine . . ." until I relent and sing it with him.

> This little light of mine, I'm gonna let it shine.
> This little light of mine, I'm gonna let it shine.
> This little light of mine, I'm gonna let it shine.
> Let it shine, let it shine, let it shine.
>
> All around the world, I'm gonna let it shine.
> All around the world, I'm gonna let it shine.
> All around the world, I'm gonna let it shine.
> Let it shine, let it shine, let it shine.
>
> This little light of mine, I'm gonna let it shine.
> This little light of mine, I'm gonna let it shine.
> This little light of mine, I'm gonna let it shine.
> Let it shine, let it shine, let it shine.

Harry sings it with abundant joy. I hope he finds plenty of ways to let his light shine in this world. I hope he never loses that joy. I hope his mother and I can help him to develop a strong sense of self, so that when he goes out into this crazy world people don't crush his joy and stomp out his light. I hope. . . .

⭐ KEY POINT

You have the perfect personality and talents to fulfill the mission God is entrusting to you.

⚡ ACTION STEP

Which of these traits most prevents you from letting your light shine? Fear, laziness, procrastination, selfishness, addiction, obsession, comparing yourself to others, allowing your critics to drain your energy and direct your life, an unwillingness to move beyond your comfort zone, self-doubt, gossip, negative relationships, worry, excuses.

(33)

Made for Mission

A lot of the dissatisfaction we experience in this lifetime comes from forgetting that we are made for mission. God didn't create us to be served; he created us to serve. If you use something for a purpose it was not designed for, things usually start to go wrong. Have you ever tried to use a snow blower as a vacuum cleaner? Right, that's a stupid idea. Have you ever tried to use a fire extinguisher to take a shower? Right, another stupid idea. Using things for something other than what they were specifically designed for usually ends up pretty ugly. But we do it with ourselves all the time.

God designed human beings for specific purposes. When we stray from them, things tend to go wrong and we start to feel dissatisfied at best and miserable at worst. You were made for mission. You will never have lasting happiness until you realize this and act on it.

For decades now, I have been speaking to people about God's dream for them to become the-best-version-of-themselves. From time to time someone will say, "Isn't that too self-focused? And if we get all focused on becoming the-best-version-of-ourselves, isn't that selfish?"

This is a common question. People ask me this all the time. Too often we think of the self as something bad. But you are profoundly good. Every time you become a-better-version-of-yourself, God can use you more powerfully for his great plans. God wants you to serve powerfully. He wants you to become the-best-version-of-yourself so you can serve more powerfully than ever before. And he wants you to become your best self because he simply delights in you.

We have spoken at length about our quest for happiness. One of the essential lessons in this quest is that we ultimately find happiness not by seeking gratification for ourselves but by serving others. You were made for mission. You were created to serve powerfully. And you will never be truly happy until you find a way to lay down your life for others that engages your talents and abilities.

"Place your talents and enthusiasm at the service of life." This was the message of Saint John Paul the Great as he traveled around the world speaking to people of all ages. Service is central to the life of a Christian. We are not the masters; we are the servants.

What are your talents? What are you really good at? How is God calling you to make the world and the Church better through those talents?

How do I discover what God is calling me to do? Ever since I began speaking and writing, this has consistently been one of the most common questions people have asked me. I have always believed that God speaks to us through our talents. He speaks to us in many other ways, but you have a unique set of talents and abilities that are God-given. Our God is a God of purpose. He does things with purpose, for purpose—one purpose. It stands to reason, then, that he gave you your particular mix of talents and abilities because they match up with the mission he has in mind for you. Of course, you cannot focus on all of your talents at one time, and you cannot fully exercise even one of your talents in this lifetime. So it is critical that we turn to God from time to time and ask, "God, which talent do you want me to focus on at this time in my life?"

Another question over the years has been, "I would like to do what you do. How do I get started?" I always begin by saying that I did not set out to do what I am doing. This work that God has called me to has evolved over time. All I have tried to do is take the next step that I believe God was asking me to take. And, of course, often I have been resistant to that next step. Often I have been lazy, afraid, and comfortable, and all these things have caused me to delay the next step. But over time you realize you will never be happy unless you take that next step, and by some grace you overcome the resistance and move forward.

Over the past couple of years I have encountered two people whose stories had a profound impact on me. The first was an elderly woman who was homebound because of a number of health issues. At Dynamic Catholic we have an extremely dedicated group of people called Mission Partners. They respond to almost every piece of incoming communication, whether that involves answering the phones, responding to letters, or replying to e-mail. The volume of incoming communication is massive and they do an outstanding job serving the people we serve by keeping up with it.

A couple of years ago one of the Mission Partners at Dynamic Catholic came to me and said, "I've got a great story for you!" She went on to explain that this elderly woman who was homebound called once a month and ordered a case of books through our low-priced bulk book program. "What does she do with the books?" I asked. This is where the story got really interesting. This is the story in her words as she told it to me when I called her the next day:

> *I woke up one day after someone had given me one of your books and CDs, and I thought to myself, "If I could live my life over again, I would do what Matthew Kelly is doing!" But I was seventy-four and homebound, so what could I do? At first I joined the Ambassador's Club and started giving ten dollars a month. That was a way for me to be involved in what you were doing. Then a couple of weeks later I woke up, and thought to myself, "I can do what Matthew Kelly is doing; I am just looking at it the wrong way." I asked myself, "What does Matthew Kelly do? He uses his talents and abilities to communicate a message to people. I can do that." It occurred to me that I had different talents and abilities. What do I have? I have time and I have the desire to share the message with others, and I had heard about the way you were distributing cheap books to get the message out to as many people as possible. So I called your organization and ordered a case of* **Rediscover Catholicism.**

When the books arrived, I sat down and wrote a letter to each of my children and grandchildren and mailed them a copy of the book with the letter. After I had done this I still had a few books left, so I did the same for some friends—a letter and a book.

One day I woke up and the case of books was empty. I was sad. I can't describe it. I called one of those lovely young people you have at Dynamic Catholic and ordered another case. When it arrived, I thought to myself, "What am I going to do with these books? Why did I even order them?"

I asked God the question, and he gave me an answer. That afternoon I was praying the Rosary and a girl I went to high school with came into my mind, so I looked her up on the Internet, and sent her a book and a letter. She sent me the most beautiful note back about three months later explaining she had been away from the Church for twenty years since her son died in a car accident, but reading my letter and the book brought her back to the Church.

From that day on each morning I asked God who he wanted me to write to today. Over the past three years I have not missed a day. I have written to every significant person in my life—friends and family, senators and congressmen and -women, movie stars and musicians, presidents of four countries, priests all over the country, and ordinary people I read about in the newspaper. It is amazing the notes and letters I get back. Sometimes they write back straightaway, but the best letters are the ones I get back a year later, after the book has really changed their lives.

I thought to myself, "Wow, what a great story. Here is a woman with every excuse under the sun not to be actively involved in ministry, but she finds a way to make it happen."

The second story is at the other end of the spectrum in some ways, but exactly the same in other ways. At an event I was doing in the corporate world I was introduced to an entrepreneur. We started talking and he said, "You know, I have been following you for ten years and I would really love to find a way to do something like what you do." Our conversation got cut short because I was introduced to give my speech, but I gave him my card and invited him to follow up with me.

About a month later he called and we arranged to meet next time I was in town. Over the past three years we have become great friends and he has become a incredible strategic partner, helping Dynamic Catholic think through some of the biggest opportunities before us.

All the time he was trying to work out how he could do full-time ministry. I asked him one day what was holding him back. He replied, "The main thing is that I have all these balls in the air for my various businesses, and so many people and their families rely on the businesses for their livelihood, and I cannot find the right person to take it all over."

I kept asking him over and over again, "What are your talents? What are you passionate about? Why do you think God gave you those talents? Why do you feel called to ministry? What in particular do you feel God is calling you to?"

We had the same conversation every six months for about three years. It was obvious he was really wrestling with these questions. But over time it became clear to me that he was not being called to full-time ministry.

What made this so clear to me were a couple of things. First, he seemed to be running away from something, rather than running toward something. Next, he was passionate about business and he was very, very good at it. And finally, he would say things like, "I feel guilty about being successful and making a lot of money," and "Business seems very worldly compared to ministry."

So we talked a lot about how as Christians we are called to be in the world, not to run away from it. We are called to elevate every environment we enter, and every honest human activity. We also talked about how important it is to have good business leaders who care about their employees rather than treat them like numbers, who pay a fair wage and run their businesses with integrity.

A few months later ran into him again, and I asked, "Are you still struggling with those questions?"

"No," he said. "I have worked all that out." I was surprised. I could tell he had, just by the way he said it.

"So, what conclusions have you come to?" I asked him.

"I've worked out that I am just really good at making money. I don't know why, but that is my primary gift. I am better at making money than anything else. You were always asking me those questions, and I wasn't being honest with myself. What are my talents? I'm good at making money. What am I passionate about? I'm passionate about my faith, I want others to get it, and I love the way Dynamic Catholic is awakening Catholics. So I have finally discerned that God gave me these passions for a reason, and he gave me my talents for a reason. And I think he just wants me to use my gifts to make a lot of money so I can give that money to Dynamic Catholic."

I smiled and he continued, "It was so simple, really, but I was complicating it. My gifts are not your gifts. Anyway, now

I am at peace. I am teaching Confirmation in my parish using DECISION POINT, and I am making money and giving it away. I have never been happier in my life."

Two stories. Two out of thousands. Ordinary people doing their own little thing in their own circle of influence. These are the people who are driving Dynamic Catholic. I wonder what your story will be.

You were made for mission. It's time to let your light shine.

⭐ KEY POINT

You cannot be happy focused on yourself. You were made for mission. It's deep within you. Only by serving others in a meaningful way do we truly discover the happiness we yearn for so unrelentingly.

⚡ ACTION STEP

What mission do you think God is calling you to now in your life? Don't get caught up in what he might have been calling you to in the past, or what he might call you to in the future. Just write down his invitation to you today as you can best discern it.

---

(34)

When God Looks at a Résumé

When you reflect on the various people God has used throughout history to carry out his work it can be quite perplexing. God often chooses the most unlikely people to carry out incredible work. Look what he did with Abraham the liar; Moses, a murderer with a speech impediment; Jeremiah in his tenderhearted youth; David the adulterer; Peter the betrayer; and Paul the Christian killer. God truly does write straight with crooked lines. And most of the time even the people God chooses are surprised that they have been chosen.

Have you ever wondered what God looks for on a résumé? Only one thing! He asks only one thing of us. He can take care of the rest. It's like what Jesus did with the five loaves and the two fish. God wants to do that with your life. The one thing God needs from you in order to launch you into mission is availability. It's the only thing he needs from any of us. Make yourself available to God and incredible things will happen.

How available are you to God at this time in your life? Twenty percent, 50 percent, 75 percent, 96.4 percent?

Talk about resistance. We are resistant to making ourselves 100 percent available to God. It's crazy when you think about it. We hold back from God because we want to be in control. This is one of the grandest delusions in human history. We are not in control, and we never will be.

Saint Ignatius of Loyola had an incredible ability to help people get beyond resistance. He was a genius at understanding human nature and how it impacts spiritual growth. This is what he wrote in *The Spiritual Exercises* about making ourselves 100 percent available to God:

> There are very few people who realize what God would make of them if they abandoned themselves entirely into his hands, and let themselves to be formed by His grace. A thick and shapeless tree trunk would never believe that it could become a statue, admired as a miracle of sculpture, and would never consent to submit itself to the chisel of the sculptor who, as Saint Augustine says, sees by his genius what he can make of it. Many people who, we see, now scarcely live as Christians, do not understand that they could become saints, if they would let themselves be formed by the grace of God, if they did not ruin His plans by resisting the work which he wants to do.

I want you to pause and consider making yourself 100 percent available to God. Try not to just read through these words. Take a minute and think about it. Ask yourself, what are you gaining by resisting

God? Is it really worth it? How much better would your life be if you surrendered completely to God? If you don't know, try not to assume that it wouldn't be any better. Ask some people you know who appear to have surrendered their life 100 percent to God. Ask them what the fruits of 100 percent availability to God are.

At the heart of the Christian experience is what our ancient Christian ancestors called conversion. God is constantly inviting us to conversion. Conversion of the heart is a daily process.

There have been several times in my spiritual journey when I have turned to God in a moment of reckless abandon and said, "Whatever you want, God. Everything is yours. I surrender to you completely. I will do whatever you want." With the perspective of time I have noticed a pattern. I pray this prayer, but then in the coming days, weeks, and months, I take everything back from God little by little. It happens so gradually that at the time I often don't even realize I am doing it.

I remember praying a prayer of complete surrender once. About ten minutes later my brother Brett asked me to borrow my golf clubs. At the time they were my single most prized possession. I had worked hard to save the money to buy them, I had agonized over buying them, and Brett was a hacker. I felt God smiling and saying, "Did you really mean what you said or were they just words?"

Why do we resist God? Because deep down we don't trust him. Why do we cast God and his ways aside? Because deep down we think that God is trying to limit our freedom.

Pope Benedict XVI gives us a powerful insight into this behavior: "The human being does not trust God. Tempted by the serpent, he harbors the suspicion that in the end, God takes something away from his life, that God is a rival who curtails our freedom and that we will be fully human only when we cast him aside. In brief, we mistakenly believe that only by casting God aside can we fully achieve our freedom."

It is time for us all to stop resisting happiness, to stop resisting the joy of life-giving daily conversion. It is time to stop resisting God. Pray for grace. Ask God. Beg him to give you the wisdom, grace, and humility to make yourself 100 percent available to him.

Let's turn to God right now and pray a prayer of transformation.

> Loving Father,
> I come to you today to make myself 100 percent available to you.
> I lay everything I have and everything I am at your feet.
> Take what you want to take,
> and give what you want to give.
> Command me in all things.
> I will do whatever you ask me to do.
> Transform me and transform my life,
> so that I may become the-very-best-version-of-myself
> and lead others to you with my life and my love!
> Amen.

★ KEY POINT
Make yourself 100 percent available to God and incredible things will happen.

⚡ ACTION STEP
Pray this prayer of transformation every day for nine days.

---

(35)

Don't Let the Critics Win

As you continue your journey, I want to encourage you to be watchful for patterns in which resistance is easily defeating you. Over the years I have noticed two in my own life.

The first surrounds critics and criticism. It is so easy to let the critic distract you from what God is calling you to do in the present moment. It is amazing how easily we can allow the critic to rob us of our passion and energy.

The critic will always be present.

I was watching a short Winnie the Pooh film online with Walter last year, and at the end of the film you had the opportunity to like or dislike it. The film had thirteen million likes and twenty-five thousand dislikes. And I thought to myself, "It is a classic story, a classic character—and what's not to like about Winnie the Pooh?" But twenty-five thousand people disliked it enough to voice their opinion. Even poor Pooh has haters.

The critics will always be there, but it is not the critic that counts. Have you ever seen a statue of a critic? No. I haven't either. Do they award any Nobel Prizes for Critic of the Year? No, there is no Best Critic Ever statue or award.

Regardless of the critic's ubiquitous presence, we need to be careful not to allow that voice too much space in our hearts and minds.

We live our lives for an audience of one: God. If you are doing what you believe God is calling you to do deep in your soul, walk on.

Throughout my life I have noticed two trends when it comes to critics. First, they have usually made up their minds before they meet you. This is quite obvious sometimes with journalists. You meet them for an interview and you can tell they have already written the story in their heads. All they are looking for are some quotes that they can chop up to serve their purpose. The second thing I find with critics is more often than not they have not read my work. They are simply reacting to something they heard from someone, which is always an oversimplification of the message, the work, and the person.

In my office at Dynamic Catholic I have a decal of these words written by Theodore Roosevelt. It spans eight feet by five feet.

> It is not the critic who counts;
> not the man who points out how the strong man stumbles,
> or where the doer of deeds could have done them better.
> The credit belongs to the man who is actually in the arena,
> whose face is marred by dust and sweat and blood;
> who strives valiantly; who errs, who comes short again and again,

because there is no effort without error and shortcoming;
but who does actually strive to do the deeds;
who knows great enthusiasms, the great devotions;
who spends himself in a worthy cause;
who at the best knows in the end the triumph of high achievement,
and who at the worst, if he fails,
at least fails while daring greatly,
so that his place shall never be with those cold and timid souls
who neither know victory nor defeat.

Be watchful. Be on guard against the critics. Resistance will use them to discourage you, or at the very least distract you. Press on with what matters most. Perseverance is the antidote for the resistance put forth by critics. It is a great virtue.

When I first started speaking at age twenty, I was taken aside by two people who were helping organize my speaking engagements. They explained to me that I should travel and speak every day. "People are fascinated because you are so young. But by the time you are twenty-five the novelty of that will be over, and then nobody will be interested in listening to you. You've got five years at the most, so speak every day. You can rest after people have lost interest in hearing you speak."

A very influential church leader told me once, "You are just dabbling in this stuff, but this is my life. And in a couple of years when you are finished dabbling with this speaking and writing, I will still be here working day after day, working to make sure the Church continues on. So as far as I am concerned, this little hobby of yours is just a distraction from the real work of the Church and the sooner you get done dabbling with it the better." Needless to say he was not a fan, and I am still "dabbling."

I have many stories like these, some much worse and not fit to print. There has been a fair share of critics and discouragers along the way. But those encouraging me have always outnumbered the critics a thousand to one. To all of those men and women, I am grateful. Your generous encouragement has helped me to defeat resistance on many days.

It has been almost twenty-five years since I published my first book. Resistance hates persistence. Perseverance is a fabulous way to slay resistance. Just keep pressing on, little by little.

When you are discouraged or caught up in procrastination, simply do the tiniest thing to move whatever you are working on forward.

Few can imagine just how powerful perseverance is. There is another quote that I like to reflect on from time to time, written by Calvin Coolidge, the thirtieth president of the United States: "Nothing in the world can take the place of persistence. Talent will not; nothing is more common than unsuccessful men with talent. Genius will not; unrewarded genius is almost a proverb. Education alone will not; the world is full of educated derelicts. Persistence and determination alone are omnipotent."

⭐ **KEY POINT**
The critics will always be there, but we need to be careful not to allow their voices too much space in our hearts and minds.

⚡ **ACTION STEP**
Reflect on a time when you allowed critics to have too much influence in your life, and how you would do it differently next time.

Blessed and Grateful

We have so much to be happy about, and it is easy to lose sight of this.

If you scan the world on any given day it very quickly becomes apparent that for all the advances we have made in medicine, technology, and food supply, there is still an overwhelming amount of suffering on this planet we call home. This suffering manifests as poverty, human trafficking, ignorance, greed, selfishness, and abuse, to name just a few.

The other day I was sitting in my office at home working and my little boy Harry came running in. He jumped up on the chair and I said to him, "How are you today, Harry?"

"I lucky boy, I very lucky boy!" he said. It made me smile. He said it with great enthusiasm and his whole little being was exuding sheer joy. It is fascinating the things their little minds grab on to. He is two and a half and I hope he always holds on to that joy.

I'm a very lucky boy too. I have lived a very fortunate life. I have been superabundantly blessed in ways that I neither understand nor deserve. Why me? Why not some child born on the same day in the Sudan who didn't live more than a week because his village had no clean water in 1973? I don't know. It is a mystery. This mystery reminds us that everything is a gift, and when you step back and truly consider it with any measure of honesty, it is all incredibly humbling.

And yet, it is not enough for us to be humbled by all the ways God has blessed us. With blessing comes responsibility. Jesus was clear when he said, "Anyone who has been given much, much will be expected of him" (Luke 12:48).

Harry's huge smile and exclamation, "I lucky boy!" is a beautiful expression of gratitude. He is too young to think about it; it just bursts out, which makes it all the more beautiful. Gratitude should always be our first response for all the blessings in our lives. Our second response should be to live a life worthy of the blessings we have received.

Without gratitude what was extraordinary yesterday becomes ordinary today. Without gratitude a sense of entitlement takes over and begins to rot our soul. Without gratitude we get old and grumpy, or even young and grumpy. Gratitude keeps us young. It anchors us to the present moment. It reminds us of what matters most and what matters least, and fills us with the resolve to carry on the great mission God has entrusted to us.

⭐ **KEY POINT**

Gratitude anchors us to the present moment, reminding us of what matters most and what matters least.

⚡ **ACTION STEP**

Count your blessings. Make a list of ten people, experiences, things, or blessings you are grateful for.

---

(37)

Never Get Discouraged

Well, here I am, at the end of the book. I have beaten resistance. I wish you could see how often I had to wrestle with it while I was writing these pages. Every day, every chapter, every section, every time my phone rang, every time I wanted to go get some chocolate... Resistance doesn't go away. But once you get into the habit of beating it, once you know you can beat it, that knowledge becomes very powerful.

You have also beaten resistance. Fifty-seven percent of books that are purchased are not read to completion. Why? Resistance. I wonder how many people will not finish this book because resistance slays them. You are not one of them. Congratulations!

Happiness is a choice. Resistance almost always stands between you and happiness. You have to break through it to experience the happiness you yearn for and the happiness God wants for you.

Thanks for reading. It is an honor to write for you. I hope that somewhere in all these words, on one of these pages, something helped you to see yourself, your life, and God in a different light, and I hope that new insight will give you the courage to stop resisting happiness.

I set out with a simple goal for this book: to give resistance a name and help you to recognize it during the moments of the day. All great stories have a villain and a hero. Resistance is the villain, and you are the hero. Have you already started recognizing the villain in your life? Simply naming resistance causes it to lose much of its power over us. Sometimes that is all you have to do, because once you name resistance in a certain situation, you recognize it for what it is and act to break through it. Resistance hates action.

Each day I pray for you, the reader, the person sitting alone somewhere, quietly considering the thoughts on these pages and the pages of the other books I have written. When I pray for you, I will be praying that you slay resistance each day.

When you do break through resistance, celebrate that, and then press on to live the life God imagined for you before the beginning of time. And if you ever feel discouraged or defeated, remember this: Every moment is a chance to start anew, a chance to turn it all around.

I hope you have enjoyed

RESISTING HAPPINESS

It has been a great privilege to write for you.
May God bless you with a prayerful spirit
and a peaceful heart.

MATTHEW KELLY

IS YOUR SOUL HUNGRY?

At Dynamic Catholic, we are passionate about feeding your soul.
Visit DynamicCatholic.com for free books, CDs, apps,
and programs! Every week we have something new to feed your soul.

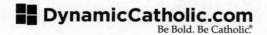

DynamicCatholic.com
Be Bold. Be Catholic.®

The Prayer Process

1 GRATITUDE

Begin by thanking God in a personal dialogue for whatever you are most grateful for today.

2 AWARENESS

Revisit the times in the past twenty-four hours when you were and were not the-best-version-of-yourself. Talk to God about these situations and what you learned from them.

3 SIGNIFICANT MOMENTS

Identify something you experienced in the last twenty-four hours and explore what God might be trying to say to you through that event (or person).

4 PEACE

Ask God to forgive you for any wrong you have committed (against yourself, another person, or Him) and to fill you with a deep and abiding peace.

5 FREEDOM:

Speak with God about how He is inviting you to change your life, so that you can experience the freedom to be the-best-version-of-yourself.

6 OTHERS:

Lift up to God anyone you feel called to pray for today, asking God to bless and guide them.

7 PRAY THE *OUR FATHER*.

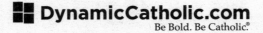

DynamicCatholic.com
Be Bold. Be Catholic.®